Interpreting
the Beatitudes

Interpreting
the Beatitudes

by

IRVIN W. BATDORF

THE WESTMINSTER PRESS
Philadelphia

Copyright © MCMLXVI W. L. Jenkins

Scripture quotations from the Revised Standard Version of the Bible are copyright, 1946
and 1952, by the Division of Christian Edu-
cation of the National Council of Churches,
and are used by permission.

LIBRARY OF CONGRESS CATALOG CARD NO. 66-11518

Published by The Westminster Press ®
Philadelphia, Pennsylvania

PRINTED IN THE UNITED STATES OF AMERICA

FOR
Doris, Marcia, and Jennifer

Contents

Preface   11

I. The Beatitudes Today:
   Three Unanswered Questions   13

      Which Evangelist Should We Follow?   13
      Can We Get Back to Jesus?   15
      Did Jesus Intend the Beatitudes Only
         for His Disciples?   17
      Bibliography   19

II. The Beatitudes in Matthew: God's Chosen
    Leader Addresses His People   21

      Who Is This Man on the Mount?   21
      What Has He Done?   23
      What Will He Say?   24
      Matthew's Total Pattern   25
      The Beatitudes of Matthew in Their
         "Natural Habitat"   27
      From Structure to Words:
         A New Dimension   29
      "The Kingdom of Heaven":
         A Matthean Favorite   31
      God's Chosen Leader Addresses His
         People: A Summing Up   32

A Postscript Concerning Exegesis   34
Bibliography   34

III. The Beatitudes in Luke: Royal Proclamation
     in Salvation History   37

Blessed Are You Poor   37
The Beatitudes as Proclamation   38
The Beatitudes as Proclamation
     to All Israel   39
Proclamation and Salvation History:
     The Purpose of Luke-Acts   40
Proclamation and the Structure
     of Luke's Gospel   43
The Beatitudes in Their "Natural
     Habitat" as Salvation History   45
Another Postscript for the Interpreter   47

IV. The Raw Materials from
    the Christian Tradition   49

The Beatitudes in Matthew's Special
     Material (Sometimes Called M)   49
The Beatitudes in Q, the Material
     Available to Both Matthew and Luke   51
The Beatitudes in Matthew's Sermon
     on the Mount   53
The Beatitude on Persecution   54
The Woes of Luke   55
The Beatitudes and Jesus   58
A Postscript on the Oral Tradition   58
Bibliography   61

V. The Raw Materials
   from Contemporary Judaism   64

Words, Words, Words   64
The Poor in the Old Testament   65

From the Old Testament to the New   68
The Poor Apart from Qumran   70
The Poor at Qumran   71
Qumran and the Beatitudes   74
The Old Testament, Qumran, and Jesus   75
Notes   81
Bibliography   82

VI. The Beatitudes in the Teaching of Jesus   85

The Kingdom of God   85
The Crisis Now:
    God Offers Himself Anew   87
The Crisis Now:
    God Demands Radical Obedience   93
The Crisis Now and the Crisis to Come   99
The Judgment to Come   104
Mercy for the Gentiles   107
The Great Reversal   110
The Son of Man   112
The Beatitudes in the Teaching of Jesus   119
Bibliography   122

VII. The Interpreter's Stance: His Angle of Vision   125

Eschatology and Existentialism
    in Bultmann   125
The Challenge of the New Quest   126
The New Hermeneutic   134
Luther and Wesley   136
Three Unanswered Questions
    Once Again   141
Notes   144
Bibliography   145

VIII. Some Axioms for Modern Preaching   149

    For the Social Order:
        A Word of Judgment   150
    For the Committed: An Invitation
        to Obey and to Hope   155
    For the Interpreter: A Word of Caution   157

Preface

WHILE THE FRUITS OF BIBLICAL SCHOLARSHIP HAVE BEEN
made available to the church in profusion, very little has
been done to explain to the average layman the methods by
which professional scholars carry on their work, so that
those for whose sake this research is being done are often
unable or unwilling to appropriate the riches laid before
them. The essay that follows attempts to bridge this gulf
between the study and the pew. While it argues for a certain interpretation of the Beatitudes, its major purpose is
to make clear how this interpretation emerges from a consistent use of the historical method. It is an exegetical
primer for concerned Christians. It is offered in the hope
that those who count themselves beginners in Biblical
study not only may come to understand how such study
should be pursued but may be inspired to make a fresh
start in it for themselves.

The word "exegesis" is derived from two Greek words,
ek and *agein,* meaning " to lead out." When used to define
the task of Biblical scholarship, it emphasizes the necessity
of leading out from the text what is actually there rather
than putting into it something foreign to its original intention. Biblical exegesis attempts to draw from the Biblical text the primary meaning its author wished to convey
to his readers. Giving priority to this ancient history, the
actual situation out of which the text arose, exegesis de-

mands that the modern interpreter think and feel his way into the mind-set and the life purpose this situation reveals by exposing himself as broadly as possible to source materials contemporary with it. The study that follows seeks to demonstrate by example how this may be done. By narrowing our focus to the Beatitudes we have been able to concentrate on particular problems and to treat in a systematic fashion the various types of primary source materials (both Christian and Jewish) to which historical method must appeal for their solution. We have insisted on understanding the message of the New Testament in its ancient setting before attempting to retranslate it into our own idiom and have arranged our chapters in such an order as would undergird this intention. There can be no axioms for preaching (Chapter VIII) until we have dealt faithfully with Jesus (Chapter VI) and we cannot deal faithfully with Jesus apart from Matthew, Luke, their predecessors, and Qumran (Chapters II–V).

Particular thanks are due to President Emeritus Walter N. Roberts, of United Theological Seminary, for arranging for me to have the time necessary for the writing of these pages. What my colleagues on the faculty had to endure by way of assuming obligations on my behalf while I was writing only they know. Above all, I stand in permanent debt to Amos Wilder, by whose kindly wisdom the particular subjects treated here were illuminated in a year of postdoctoral study at Harvard, and to Otto Piper of Princeton, without whose penetrating concern for both me and the New Testament my pilgrimage as a scholar would never have begun.

I. W. B.

I · The Beatitudes Today:
Three Unanswered Questions

NO PORTION OF HOLY WRIT IS SO HIGHLY PRAISED BUT SO little practiced as the Sermon on the Mount. And no part of the Sermon is so widely quoted but so poorly understood as the Beatitudes. The reason for this lies not simply in us, but in the text itself. Three unanswered questions block our way.

WHICH EVANGELIST SHOULD WE FOLLOW?

The choice demanded of us is painfully clear when we set down in parallel columns Matt. 5:3-12 and Luke 6:20-26, italicizing only those words about which the two Evangelists show exact agreement.

Matthew, ch. 5	*Luke, ch. 6*
8 *Blessed are* the *poor* in spirit, *for* theirs *is the kingdom of* heaven.	20 *Blessed are you poor, for* yours *is the kingdom of* God.
4 *Blessed are* those who mourn, *for* they shall be comforted.	21b *Blessed are* you that weep now, *for* you shall laugh.
5 Blessed are the meek, for they shall inherit the earth.	

Matthew, ch. 5

6 *Blessed are* those who *hunger* and thirst for righteousness, *for* they *shall be satisfied.*

7 Blessed are the merciful, for they shall obtain mercy.

8 Blessed are the pure in heart, for they shall see God.

9 Blessed are the peacemakers, for they shall be called sons of God.

10 Blessed are those who are persecuted for righteousness' sake, for theirs is the kingdom of heaven.

11 *Blessed are you when men revile you and* persecute you and utter all kinds of *evil* against you falsely *on* my *account.*

12 *Rejoice* and be glad, *for your reward is great in heaven, for so* men persecuted *the prophets* who were before you.

Luke, ch. 6

21a *Blessed are* you that *hunger* now, *for* you *shall be satisfied.*

22 *Blessed are you when men* hate you, and when they exclude you and *revile you, and* cast out your name as *evil, on account* of the Son of man!

23 *Rejoice* in that day, and leap for joy, *for* behold, *your reward is great in heaven; for so* their fathers did to *the prophets.*

24 But woe to you that are rich, for you have received your consolation.

Luke, ch. 6

²⁵ Woe to you that are full now, for you shall hunger. Woe to you that laugh now, for you shall mourn and weep.

²⁶ Woe to you, when all men speak well of you, for so their fathers did to the false prophets.

If there is little agreement, there is also much disagreement. Matthew has five Beatitudes that do not occur in Luke, and Luke has four Woes that do not appear in Matthew. Where there are some likenesses, the differences stand out all the more.

Matthew	Luke
kingdom of heaven	kingdom of God
poor in spirit	poor
mourn — comfort	weep now — laugh
hunger and thirst for righteousness	hunger now
persecute	hate — exclude
utter . . . against you falsely	cast out your name as evil
on my account	on account of the Son of man
rejoice and be glad	rejoice in that day and leap for joy
men persecuted the prophets who were before you	their fathers did to the prophets

CAN WE GET BACK TO JESUS?

The question must be stated in this bold fashion since the differences we have observed between Matthew and Luke are typical of the whole Gospel record. If we are

puzzled to know which version of the Beatitudes best expresses the mind of Jesus, many another passage brings us
equal puzzlement. Which version of the Lord's Prayer may
we ascribe to Jesus (Matt. 6:9-13; Luke 11:2-4)? Did he
tell his parables in order to blind his hearers, or was their
blindness their own doing? Matthew and Mark offer different answers (Mark 4:11-12; Matt. 13:11-15)! Did Jesus
cleanse the Temple at the beginning of his ministry (John
2:13-22) or at the end (Mark 11:15-19)? Was his last meal
with the disciples a Passover (Mark 14:12) or did it occur
before the Passover (John 13:1; 18:28)? As we ponder
such persistent questions we are led to see that the Gospels
were not written to supply the kind of information about
Jesus that we would like to have. They are biographical
only in a very limited sense. They give us a portrait of
Jesus but not a photographic reproduction.

The reason for this apparent lack of precision is twofold. On the one hand, the only records available to the
Evangelists came to them not by way of a printing press
but by word of mouth, molded not by modern laws of
copyright but by patterns of transmission inherited from
the interpreters and teachers of ancient Judaism. On the
other hand, those who wrote down Jesus' story knew him
not simply as a figure of the immediate past but as their
own living Shepherd. They preserved the history of Jesus'
words and deeds in order to herald his triumph as risen
Lord. They received the raw materials for their task from
the community gathered by his resurrection power. They
wrote at his personal command both to sustain that community and to forward its mission in the world. As with
Paul the good news they proclaim is " revealed through
faith for faith " (Rom. 1:17). What they provide for us is
not mere factual reporting but a post-resurrection reinterpretation intended to sustain faith in the one who had
been raised. So we read in John 20:30-31, " Now Jesus did
many other signs in the presence of the disciples, which are

not written in this book; but these are written that you may believe that Jesus is the Christ, the Son of God, and that believing you may have life in his name."

Although all four Evangelists take this standpoint, they develop its meaning in different ways. John sees in every event of Jesus' earthly life a revelation of his divine glory (John 2:1-11). Mark tells a breathtaking tale whose unpredictable outcome is the revelation of Jesus' glory only to his chosen twelve at Caesarea Philippi (Mark 8:27-30; 9:2-9). Matthew marshals each event of Jesus' life to prove from the Old Testament that he both had fulfilled and would fulfill his divine role as risen Savior and Judge (Matt. 4:12-17; 12:15-21; 28:16-20). Whereas Matthew moves freely and without warning from a pre-resurrection event to its post-resurrection result (Matt. 16:17-20), Luke, as a meticulous craftsman, deliberately builds the resurrection into the basic structure of his account by allowing it to separate the period of Jesus from that of the church (Luke 1:1-4; 24:24-27, 44-52; Acts 1:1-11).

Although it would seem obligatory to take such ancient reinterpretation seriously, few modern interpreters of the Beatitudes really do so. Bishop Gore felt at the turn of the century that Jesus spoke both versions of each Beatitude on different occasions. For John Wick Bowman some fifty years later Jesus himself combined the source material still visible in Matthew's Beatitudes so that the finished product might describe the successive stages of growth through which a maturing disciple ought to progress.

DID JESUS INTEND THE BEATITUDES ONLY FOR HIS DISCIPLES?

This question arises as soon as we take seriously the difference between the " poor " and the " poor in spirit," between " those who hunger and thirst for righteousness " and those who simply hunger. Did Jesus address himself

to moral virtue or solely to human need? If only the
hungry and the dispossessed had marched from Selma to
Montgomery, Malcolm X would have found himself in
good company. As it turned out the day was won by the
poor in spirit, and we could all thank God once more that
the Spirit of his Son had been at work in the Negro revolu-
tion of our time.

If we consult the bibliography at the end of this chapter,
we shall find that modern writers differ sharply in their
answer to this third question. Some writers transform the
Beatitudes into *general principles of conduct,* as though
it mattered very little who had spoken them first or to
whom they were being addressed. This is particularly evident in the psychological use to which the Beatitudes are
put by Ernest M. Ligon and the philosophical form given
them by Gerald Heard. The latter makes of them an eight-
fold ladder to spiritual perfection that can be ascended by
any reasonable man who practices purgation and gains
spiritual proficiency, whether Buddhist or Christian. In a
similar but more subdued vein such Christian statesmen as
Bishop Gore, E. Stanley Jones, and C. F. Andrews look
upon the Beatitudes as common ground to be shared by
Hindu and Christian alike. Here in America such prominent leaders as Ralph Sockman, Charles R. Brown, or
Robert H. Miller make the Beatitudes the basis of their
appeal to non-Christians. In this context the Beatitudes
appear as spiritual principles whose adoption will bring
personal fulfillment and social justice. Although Jesus exemplified these principles best of all and their full practice puts one in his company, the fact that they arose as
Beatitudes in his ministry in Palestine is secondary.

Other writers disagree sharply, contending that the
Beatitudes can only be interpreted as *the birthright of
Christian faith.* This is particularly true of Thurneysen,
Bonhoeffer, and Thielicke, for whom the Beatitudes con-
vey only to Christians the promises of the risen Lord. In a

somewhat different but equally positive way Jeremias, Hunter, and Dibelius root the Beatitudes in Christian experience. For the Catholic, Jules Lebreton, they sketch the goal of moral virtue for the Christian elite.

BIBLIOGRAPHY

THE BEATITUDES TODAY: A SELECTED BIBLIOGRAPHY

Andrews, Charles F., *The Sermon on the Mount*. The Macmillan Company, 1942.

Atkins, Gaius G., *From the Hillside*. The Pilgrim Press, 1948.

Baker, Eric, *The Neglected Factor*. Abingdon Press, 1963.

*Bonhoeffer, Dietrich, *The Cost of Discipleship*, tr. by R. H. Fuller, 2d ed., revised. The Macmillan Company, 1959.

*Bowman, John Wick, and Tapp, Roland W., *The Gospel from the Mount*. The Westminster Press, 1957.

Brown, C. R., *The Religion of a Layman*. The Macmillan Company, 1921.

Chappell, C. G., *The Sermon on the Mount*. Cokesbury Press, 1930.

Dibelius, Martin, *The Sermon on the Mount*. Charles Scribner's Sons, 1940.

Fox, Emmet, *The Sermon on the Mount*. Harper & Brothers, 1938.

Gore, Charles, *The Sermon on the Mount*. London: John Murray, 1899.

Graham, William F., *The Secret of Happiness*. Doubleday & Company, Inc., 1955.

Heard, Gerald, *The Code of Christ*. Harper & Brothers, 1941.

*Hunter, Archibald M., *A Pattern for Life: An Exposition of the Sermon on the Mount* (Revised Edition). The Westminster Press, 1966.

*Jeremias, Joachim, *The Sermon on the Mount*, tr. by Norman Perrin. Facet Books. Fortress Press, 1963.

Jones, E. Stanley, *The Christ of the Mount*. Abingdon Press, 1931.

*Suitable as textbooks for group Bible study in the local church.

*Kepler, Thomas S., *Jesus' Design for Living*. Abingdon Press, 1955.

Lebreton, Jules, *The Spiritual Teaching of the New Testament*, tr. by James Whalen. Newman Press, 1960.

Ligon, Ernest M., *The Psychology of Christian Personality*. The Macmillan Company, 1935.

*Martin, Hugh, *The Beatitudes*. Harper & Brothers, 1953.

Miller, Robert H., *The Life Portrayed in the Sermon on the Mount*. W. A. Wilde Company, 1934.

Montizambert, Eric, *The Flame of Life*. The Seabury Press, Inc., 1955.

Russell, E., *The Beatitudes*. Doubleday, Doran and Company, Inc., 1929.

*Shinn, Roger L., *The Sermon on the Mount*. United Church Press, 1962.

*Sockman, Ralph W., *The Higher Happiness*. Apex Books. Abingdon-Cokesbury Press, 1950.

Stamm, Frederick K., *Seeing the Multitudes*. Harper & Brothers, 1943.

Thielicke, Helmut, *Life Can Begin Again*, tr. by John W. Doberstein. Fortress Press, 1963.

*Thompson, Ernest T., *The Sermon on the Mount and Its Meaning for Today*, rev. ed. Aletheia Paperback. John Knox Press, 1961.

*Thurneysen, Eduard, *The Sermon on the Mount*, tr. by W. C. Robinson and J. M. Robinson. Chime Paperback. John Knox Press, 1964.

Vann, Gerald, *The Divine Pity: Social Implications of the Beatitudes*. Image Book, D 109. Doubleday & Company, Inc., 1961.

Watcyn-Williams, M., *The Beatitudes in the Modern World*. The Round Table Press, n.d.

Windisch, Hans, *The Meaning of the Sermon on the Mount*, tr. by S. MacLean Gilmour. The Westminster Press, 1951.

Wright, T. H., *The Sermon on the Mount for Today*. Edinburgh: T. & T. Clark, 1927.

*Suitable as textbooks for group Bible study in the local church.

II · The Beatitudes in Matthew: God's Chosen Leader Addresses His People

AS ANYONE CAN SEE WITH HALF AN EYE, THE BEATITUDES were delivered by Jesus on what Matthew regards as an important occasion. Jesus was seated. He was on a mountain. His disciples had come for instruction. Not far off, as if to overhear, were the " great crowds " drawn from every corner of the Holy Land by Jesus' preaching, teaching, and healing. Nor does this auspicious occasion come by chance or without preparation. It is a summit to which Matthew leads us step by step through his first four chapters by portraying with meticulous care the man who finally sits there to teach. According to Matthew, what Jesus says must be interpreted in the light of what he has done and will do. The man and the mount go together.

Who Is This Man on the Mount?

Who this man is Matthew loses no time in declaring. His whole Gospel is at bottom a book about Jesus. He speaks not simply about Jesus' character or friends or influence but about the task given him by God. He explains Jesus' function as the agent of God's purpose.

Even the name " Jesus Christ " (Matt. 1:1) defines this task. In this sense it is a functional name. " Jesus " in Hebrew means " Savior." " Christ " in Greek means " Anointed One " and is the equivalent of the Hebrew

" Messiah." When " Jesus " is called " Christ " or " Messiah," these titles describe the task given him by God. He is the one anointed by God to save his people from their sins (v. 21).

Matthew's elaborate genealogy teaches the same lesson. By using a schematic pattern to speak to Jewish people in a Jewish way (ch. 1:1, 17) Matthew sets Jesus at the very apex of Jewish history. Since he is anointed to save God's people from their sins, his life is the culmination of their history. It is supremely appropriate that he should rank with Abraham and David since he is the one who brings their work to its appointed fruition in the unfolding of God's purpose.

Jesus' name and his genealogy reflect Matthew's profound reading of the Old Testament, and it is this that undergirds the whole of his infancy narratives. Since Jesus is born of a virgin according to the word of Isaiah (Matt. 1:23), we know that he is the one appointed by God to bring Isaiah's prophecy to fruition. That Jesus should be born in Bethlehem, or flee to Egypt, or spark a massacre, or dwell in Nazareth would have the same meaning (ch. 2:6, 15, 18, 23). In each case an incident from Jesus' history is set by Matthew in an Old Testament frame to show how it points beyond itself to what God is doing through him. If Matthew can find some Old Testament text in which the events of Jesus' life are mirrored, it is proof enough for him that God is indeed at work. Although this rabbinic method of adducing " proof " is understandably difficult for us to follow, it need not blind us to the reality Matthew desires to illumine. Whatever happens to Jesus, even as a tiny baby unable to do or say anything on his own, reveals how powerfully God acts to effect his ancient promise. Since God's ultimate purpose is to minister to the whole world, Matthew brings to Jesus' cradle three Gentile kings. As God the creator is able to bring strength out of weakness, so he preserves the baby Jesus in spite of Herod's rage. While Herod trembles, these Wise Men from afar not only bring gifts fit for a king but risk their own kingly necks on Jesus' behalf. As Jesus will later rule from his cross, so even now he controls all these bewildering and tragic events from his cradle (ch. 2:1-12). As Matthew has been taught, so he teaches us. Jesus is indeed the Messiah.

WHAT HAS HE DONE?

The events that Matthew now sets forth (Matt. 3:1 to 4:25) serve as a frontispiece to announce the kind of story that he has in store for us. The deeds chronicled in this short section are not simple biography but typical Messianic history. When Jesus accepts the baptism of John (ch. 3:1-17), he does so not to confess his own sins but again functionally as God's Son to " fulfill all righteousness " (v. 15). The Voice from heaven and the descent of the Spirit do not indicate for Jesus what we would call an " uplifting experience," but the entrance of God himself into the history of his people according to the pattern revealed in Ps. 2 and Isa., ch. 42. The period of " temptation " (Matt. 4:1-11) is a testing not just for this particular moment, but one required by the lifelong commitments that Jesus' Messianic function has already put upon him. His adversary is Satan himself. Each typical test is based upon the use to which Jesus will put his Messianic power. Will he, as God's Son, fight God's battles with God's weapons or will he rely on himself alone? In each case Jesus decides for God on the basis of God's word.

In so acting, he acts not for himself alone but as the leader of God's people. Like them, he is in the wilderness. Their forty years (Deut. 8:1-3) become for him forty days and forty nights. As they were given manna and water (vs. 15-16), so he receives the ministry of angels. As a Jewish Messiah, Jesus must nevertheless bring light to the Gentiles (Matt. 4:12-16). As the one of whom John had spoken, he

must now take up the message that John is no longer able
to give (vs. 12, 17). As the Son of God, freshly anointed
by his Spirit, he is able to call disciples with sovereign freedom and to expect the immediate response he in fact elicits
from Peter, Andrew, James, and John (vs. 18-22). He will
call men to himself, train them, and send them forth,
basing his hope for their success solely on what they can
learn from him. What follows is what Matthew has led us
to expect would follow from the sovereign efforts of so
mighty a Messiah. To taste his preaching, teaching, and
healing, throngs crowd in upon him, not only from the
length and breadth of the Holy Land but from " all Syria "
as well (vs. 23-25).

What Will He Say?

Unless we now use this pathway which Matthew has prepared to approach his mountain we will not hear what is
said from it. We have no right to read Matthew's fifth
chapter as though chapters one to four had not been
written. With the perspective they provide we can see
that Jesus is no humble Galilean peasant moving incognito
among his countrymen. The voice we hear is that of the
risen Lord speaking to those whom his resurrection power
has gathered.

Matthew 5:1-16. Jesus begins with the Beatitudes whose
promises and demands picture what role his disciples are
to play in the world. Like the Messiah, the Messianic people must expect persecution, but, like the Messiah, they
will be salt and light.

Matthew 5:17 to 6:18. Jesus makes clear that he has come
not to destroy the law but to fulfill it (ch. 5:17-18) and
that this mission places certain obligations on his disciples
(vs. 19-48). Where the law had said " no murder," he says
" no anger." Where the law had said " no adultery," he
forbids even the lustful look. Where the law had permitted

divorce under certain conditions, he forbids it entirely except in one circumstance. Where the law permitted oaths, he recommends utter simplicity of speech. Where the law had sanctioned retaliation, he commands his disciples to turn the other cheek. Where the law had required the love of neighbor, Jesus says, " Love your enemies." Beyond these six so-called " antitheses " come three other antithetical statements that Jesus sets forth in contrast to the " pillars " of Pharisaic piety (ch. 6:1-18), so that the righteousness of the church might actually exceed that of the synagogue (ch. 5:20). The church may not forget alms, prayer, and fasting, but her alms must be in secret, her prayer without hypocrisy, and her fasting with joy.

Matthew 6:19 to 7:27. In one final section Jesus deals very personally with the decisions his disciples must make in order to demonstrate in explicit ways how fully they really do belong to him. As their Lord, he commands, he prohibits, and he gives solemn warning. His disciples must keep mammon in check (ch. 6:19-34). They must not be censorious (ch. 7:1-5), nor unwise (v. 6), but always open toward God (vs. 7-11) and charitable toward men (v. 12). They must choose the narrow way (vs. 13-14), reject false prophets whose fruit is bad (vs. 15-20), and themselves produce the good fruits of obedience (vs. 21-27).

Matthew's Total Pattern

We have now analyzed the first seven chapters of Matthew by calling attention to the man on the mount and asking who he is, what he does, and what he says. By so doing we have also uncovered the Messianic pattern of Matthew's entire work. We must remind ourselves once more that the word " Messiah " or " Anointed One " was a Jewish title intended to describe the leader God would choose and send for the salvation of his people. It is precisely this person whom Matthew claims to have discovered in Jesus. His story about Jesus is Messianic because it exhibits what Jesus said and did to fulfill this ancient promise God had made to his people. Only now the church takes the place of Israel as the new people of God, and Jesus acts on her behalf.

As Messiah, Jesus delivers five major discourses to these very people. Each discourse is preceded by a narrative that reveals the power Jesus wields in what he does as Messiah. Each discourse then explains how Jesus' deeds have created a new pattern of conduct in which his disciples must walk if they would belong to him, their life as God's new people depending solely on him. Each discourse brings forth a major topic of central importance for both the historical life of Jesus and the later experience of the church. That there are five such topics prior to the passion story itself has led many interpreters to compare these five " books " of Matthew with the Pentateuch. The Evangelist would then be suggesting by the very structure of his work that Jesus is a new Moses giving a new law to a new Israel. His intention becomes crystal clear when this structure is reduced to outline form.

Section One — DISCIPLESHIP

Narrative: The birth and preparation
               of the Messiah.   Chs. 1:1 to 4:25
Discourse: The Messiah gives a new law
               to his people.   Chs. 5:1 to 7:29

Section Two — APOSTLESHIP

Narrative: The Messiah fulfills his mis-
               sion by mighty works.   Chs. 8:1 to 9:34
Discourse: The Messiah gives a new
               mission to his people.   Chs. 9:35 to 11:1

Section Three — REVELATION AND RESPONSE

Narrative: The Messiah revealed but
               rejected.   Chs. 11:2 to 12:50

| *Discourse:* | The Kingdom hidden and revealed in the Messiah's parabolic teaching. | Ch. 13 |

Section Four — THE CHURCH

| *Narrative:* | The Messiah gathers his people. | Chs. 14:1 to 17:27 |
| *Discourse:* | The Messiah instructs his people in church "discipline." | Chs. 18:1 to 19:2 |

Section Five — THE GOAL OF SALVATION

| *Narrative:* | The Messiah in Jerusalem for his final conflict. | Chs. 19:3 to 23:39 |
| *Discourse:* | The Messiah prepares his people for the Parousia. | Chs. 24:1 to 26:1 |

Section Six — DEATH AND RESURRECTION

| *Narrative:* | The Messiah dies but rises again. | Chs. 26:2 to 28:15 |
| *Discourse:* | The Messiah commissions his people anew. | Ch. 28:16-20 |

THE BEATITUDES OF MATTHEW IN THEIR "NATURAL HABITAT"

It should be obvious from the outline of Matthew's structure that the Beatitudes stand at the forefront of Jesus' first discourse. What purpose had the Evangelist in giving them so prominent a place? As we have noted, each discourse picks up some element in Jesus' ministry that has continuing relevance for Matthew's readers. In this instance the subject is discipleship itself. It is this concern that binds each discourse to the narrative preceding it. It is this concern that binds the Gospel as a whole to the church whose life it sustains. Little wonder that it is also this concern to which Matthew gives priority. Once the reader accepts what the Evangelist urges here, all the rest falls into line. Once reject what Matthew urges here and there is no point in reading further. If Jesus is the Messiah and his life on earth really does set the pattern that his disciples should match, then his words here and in all the following discourses make sense. If this is not so, then the bottom drops out of Matthew's whole argument. *In this light* the Beatitudes become the *hinge* upon which the whole of Matthew's structure turns. They characterize discipleship once and for all. They epitomize its demands with unerring precision.

How firmly this joins the Beatitudes to Jesus we shall have occasion to ponder time and again. As we saw in Chapter I, many modern writers treat the Beatitudes as general principles of conduct and put no stress on their origin in the ministry of Jesus. They point out that it is only at Matt. 5:11 that allegiance to Jesus is first specifically called for, and they reason on this basis that the Beatitudes only relate men to God but not necessarily to Jesus. But such an interpretation overlooks completely the central place occupied by the Beatitudes as the hinge upon which Matthew's structure turns. When we see ch. 5 in the light of what precedes and follows it, we cannot separate its blessing from the new life released by Jesus' death and resurrection.

As modern interpreters, we impulsively tend to uproot the Beatitudes from this soil in which Matthew has planted them. We treat them as though they were spoken long ago by an ancient teacher to every living soul. Since this is our view of the Beatitudes, we feel free to separate their teaching from the teacher and to use whatever suits our fancy or need. But for Matthew, Jesus is no dead teacher, nor is he speaking to all men, nor is he addressing men individually one by one. Rather, in Matthew's view, Jesus is the risen Lord speaking to the whole of his gathered flock. As he puts it in another passage (ch. 11:29), "Take my yoke upon you, and learn from me; for I am gentle and lowly in heart, and you will find rest for your souls." Since in this habitat the Beatitudes belong only to Jesus' disciples, Matthew speaks clearly to the third question that was posed in Chapter I.

From Structure to Words: A New Dimension

Every New Testament text can be entered by more than one door. We open another such door when we turn from the overall structure of this Gospel to its vocabulary. If the words we use betray our way of life, the same is true of Matthew. Each of his words comes to us laden with the treasure he once put there. Since it is all too easy to confuse our ideas with those of Matthew, we must listen carefully for his particular accent. If we think, for example, about such words as " righteousness " or " meek " or " kingdom of heaven," we instinctively fill them with all kinds of special meanings rising from our own experience. The task before us is to separate the meanings we put into Matthew's words from the very special cargo he himself placed on board when he first started them on their way.

By listing the words that Matthew employs in our particular passage and checking his use of them elsewhere, we come closer to understanding what he says all around. But to find out where any one word occurs in the whole of Matthew we need to use a Bible concordance. With such information we may judge for ourselves whether the sense of any one word, such as " righteousness," for example, varies from passage to passage within Matthew itself (consult chs. 3:15; 5:6, 10, 20; 6:1, 33; 21:32) .

We may then go one step farther by comparing how Matthew, Mark, and Luke use any one word. This second step is made possible by turning to *Gospel Parallels,* a tool for Bible study that arranges corresponding passages of Matthew, Mark, and Luke in parallel columns to facilitate

easy comparison. Both of these steps, first with the concordance and then with *Gospel Parallels,* are within the
reach of every student. As a matter of fact, the next section is an open invitation to every reader to use these tools
on his own in connection with the word " blessed." Do it
first for yourself and then check your results with what
follows.

When Jesus is asked who he is, he responds, " And
blessed is he who takes no offense at me " (ch. 11:6). Similarly blessed are Jesus' disciples, " But blessed are your
eyes, for they see, and your ears, for they hear " (ch.
13:16). This is also Peter's situation on confessing Jesus
as the Christ. " Blessed are you, Simon Bar-Jona! For flesh
and blood has not revealed this to you, but my Father who
is in heaven " (ch. 16:17). To those awaiting his Parousia
Jesus says, " Blessed is that servant whom his master when
he comes will find so doing " (ch. 24:46). Quite clearly
" blessed " is a discipleship word, and Matthew uses it to
describe a disciple's lot both before (chs. 16:17; 13:16;
11:6) and after the resurrection (ch. 24:46).

If we now use *Young's Analytical Concordance* or a good
Greek concordance, we find that the Greek word translated
by " blessed " in Matt. 5:3-11 is *makarios.* In the Gospels
this word occurs only in Matthew, Luke, and John (John
13:17; 20:29). When we consult the material in *Gospel
Parallels* that Matthew and Luke have in common (paragraphs 64, 92, 226), the word-for-word likeness is so exact
that it is probable both Gospels were drawing here on a
prior source (usually designated by the letter Q).

We conclude that Matthew's use of *makarios* as a discipleship word with quite broad connotations is not peculiar to the First Gospel but represents a usage already
prevalent in early Christendom. Not simply for Matthew
but for Luke, Q, and John, blessing comes by obedience
to Jesus the Christ.

"THE KINGDOM OF HEAVEN": A MATTHEAN FAVORITE

Our tabulation from the concordance is easily set down.

Matthew uses "kingdom of heaven"	32 times
"kingdom" alone	10 times
"kingdom of God"	4 times
"kingdom," with other designations than "heaven" or "God"	5 times

Judging just from Matthew alone, "kingdom of heaven" is obviously a Matthean favorite. Beyond this, as the concordance also shows, this phrase does not occur anywhere else. "Kingdom of heaven" is thus an exclusively Matthean expression. When we peruse those passages where it occurs in *Gospel Parallels* we have one other indication of Matthew's special bias. Only twice does he use "kingdom of God" on his own (ch. 21:31 and 43), and only twice where it has parallels with either Mark or Luke (chs. 12:28; 19:24). But there are twelve passages in which Matthew uses "kingdom of heaven" in preference to "kingdom of God" as this occurs in the corresponding sections of either Mark or Luke (chs. 4:17; 5:3; 8:11; 10:7; 11:11, 12; 13:11, 31, 33; 18:3; 19:14, 23). We could hardly find a phrase that in itself might give such promising entrance into the mind of the Evangelist as this.

As it turns out, we are not disappointed, for Matthew's use of this phrase does indeed demonstrate the situation in which he stands with relation to the church and to Jesus. As we reminded ourselves in the last chapter, the church first kept her records of Jesus in order to support her proclamation of him as risen Lord. The documents that the Evangelists produced thus reveal a double perspective. They tell us not only about what the man Jesus did and said but also how he was constantly directing the life of the church as her exalted Savior. Thus Matthew's first

discourse is Jesus' interpretation of the law for the edifica-
tion of Matthew's readers with particular reference to
their conflict with the synagogue. This is clearly evident,
for example, in Matt. 5:11-12, 17-20; and 6:1-18. Matthew's second discourse contains Jesus' marching orders
for the apostolic mission of the post-resurrection church,
built upon Jesus' original sending out of the Twelve
but going far beyond that. His fourth discourse might be
classified as a manual of discipline for the ordering of
church life. It is in keeping with this double perspective
that when this Evangelist writes " kingdom of heaven "
he thinks not only about Jesus and the Twelve but of the
pilgrimage of the church following the resurrection, in
which he himself has a major stake.

Thus " kingdom of heaven " describes the preaching of
Jesus, John the Baptist, and the church facing the Parousia
(Matt. 3:2; 11:11; 12:28; 13:11, 19, 31, 33, 44-45; 24:14).
It pertains in this latter context to the Last Judgment following the Parousia (chs. 13:36-43, 47-50; 25:1-46).
Within this broad span it is identified with the church
herself. This is explicit in the only two passages containing
the word " church " in all the Gospels (chs. 16:18; 18:17).
In the first of these, Peter, upon whom Christ builds his
church, is given " the keys of the kingdom of heaven "
(ch. 16:19). In the second instance the power of binding
and loosing is given to the church (ch. 18:17-18) in a
passage introduced by three Matthean references to the
kingdom (ch. 18:1, 3, 4). The words are ascribed to
Jesus, but the voice surely belongs to Matthew.

God's Chosen Leader Addresses His People: A Summing Up

In our study of Matthew thus far we have sought to illustrate two basic approaches to the interpretation of the
Beatitudes. First, we analyzed the whole *structure* of the

First Gospel to see the larger context in which the Beatitudes appear. Second, we sought to open up a " new dimension " by narrowing our attention to *words*. We tried to catch the meaning of the specific words used in the Beatitudes both by examining Matthew's use of them elsewhere and by comparing his usage with that of Mark and Luke.

At the end of the first step we concluded: (1) that the Beatitudes, as Matthew's first full-length portrait of discipleship, form the hinge upon which the whole of the First Gospel turns and (2) that they cannot be separated from Jesus, understood as the leader chosen by God for the formation and direction of his people. We saw that the structure of each of the five great sections of Matthew leads inevitably to these conclusions, since each assumes the Lordship of Jesus and each pictures him acting for, and giving direction to, his disciples. Matthew is conscious that the Jewish people expected God to send his anointed leader to them and he shows on the basis of many Old Testament texts that Jesus is that leader and that the church to whom he ministers is the New Israel, God's newly formed people. The Beatitudes thus become the direction of Jesus Messiah for the New Israel.

What may we conclude on the basis of our study of the word " blessed " and the famous Matthean phrase " kingdom of heaven "? When we ponder the meaning that the Evangelist gives to these words *beyond* the context of the Beatitudes, does this help us to understand the Beatitudes in their own context? Does such *word study,* limited as it has been, verify or contradict the impression we had received from our broader survey of *structure?*

On both counts the answer is clear and reassuring. (1) The Beatitudes once again appear as discipleship ethics. The word " blessed " is always applied elsewhere by Matthew to those who obey Jesus, and the " kingdom of heaven " is promised only to such people. (2) The Lordship of Jesus is once again affirmed since the " kingdom of heaven " that he heralds stretches all the way from his earliest ministry on earth to his return in glory.

So far as Matthew is concerned only one of the questions from Chapter I receives any definite answer. In his opinion the Beatitudes were meant only for Jesus' disciples. Matthew gives us no help in separating what Jesus said before his death from what he revealed to his gathered flock after he was raised up.

A POSTSCRIPT CONCERNING EXEGESIS

The word " exegesis " stems from a Greek root meaning " to lead out." We practice exegesis when we draw out from any one text the original intention of its author instead of reading into it our own ideas. We have been trying to take some first steps in this direction. We can only hope that some of our more hardy readers will carry these small beginnings much farther by working on such terms as " poor," " meek," " merciful," " righteousness," and " persecute." By using a concordance and *Gospel Parallels,* any serious student can free himself not only from his own preconceptions but also from slavish subjection to the commentaries. He can undergird his preaching and teaching with firsthand insights that will delight those to whom he ministers and feed his own soul. But the price is heavy! Independent digging must precede whatever use he finally makes of the commentaries and the theological wordbooks, where much broader vistas may be glimpsed. Luke may be studied in the same way.

BIBLIOGRAPHY

CONCORDANCES OF THE BIBLE

Nelson's Complete Concordance of the Revised Standard Version Bible. Thomas Nelson & Sons, 1957.

Young's Analytical Concordance to the Bible. Funk and Wagnalls Company, n.d.

Parallel Arrangements of the Synoptic Gospels

Burton, E., and Goodspeed, E., *A Harmony of the Synoptic Gospels for Historical and Critical Study*. Charles Scribner's Sons, 1917.

Throckmorton, Burton H. (ed.), *Gospel Parallels: A Synopsis of the First Three Gospels*, 2d ed. Thomas Nelson & Sons, 1957.

Commentaries on Matthew

Argyle, Aubrey W., *The Gospel According to Matthew* (The Cambridge Bible Commentary on the New English Bible). Cambridge: Cambridge University Press, 1963.

*Barclay, William, *The Gospel of Matthew* (The Daily Study Bible). The Westminster Press, 1959.

*Cox, George E. P., *The Gospel According to St. Matthew* (Torch Bible Commentaries). London: SCM Press, Ltd., 1952.

*Dietrich, Suzanne de, *The Gospel According to Matthew*, tr. by Donald G. Miller (The Layman's Bible Commentary, No. 16). John Knox Press, 1961.

Filson, Floyd V., *Commentary on the Gospel According to St. Matthew* (Harper's New Testament Commentaries). Harper & Brothers, 1960.

Grant, Frederick C., *Nelson's Bible Commentary Based on the Revised Standard Version*. Vol. VI: *New Testament: Matthew-Acts*. Thomas Nelson & Sons, 1962.

*Green, F. W., *The Gospel According to St. Matthew*, 2d ed. (The Clarendon Bible). Oxford: Clarendon Press, 1945.

Johnson, Sherman E., "The Gospel According to St. Matthew," *The Interpreter's Bible*, Vol. 7. Abingdon Press, 1951.

Robinson, T. H., *The Gospel of Matthew* (The Moffatt New Testament Commentary). London: Hodder and Stoughton, Ltd., 1928.

Tasker, Randolph V. G., *The Gospel According to St. Matthew* (The Tyndale New Testament Commentaries). Wm. B. Eerdmans Publishing Company, 1961.

*Suitable for group Bible study in the local church.

STUDIES IN THE GOSPELS

*Barrett, C. K., *Luke the Historian in Recent Study*. Alec R. Allenson, Inc., 1961. Highly readable survey by noted scholar.

*Blair, Edward P., *Jesus in the Gospel of Matthew*. Abingdon Press, 1960.

Cadbury, Henry J., *The Making of Luke-Acts*. Alec R. Allenson, Inc., 1958. The reprint of a classic, first issued in 1927.

Conzelmann, Hans, *The Theology of St. Luke,* tr. by Geoffrey Buswell. Harper & Brothers, 1960. Basic to modern discussion, but difficult to read.

Franzmann, Martin H., *Follow Me: Discipleship According to Saint Matthew*. Concordia Publishing House, 1961.

*Fuller, Reginald H., *Luke's Witness to Jesus Christ* (World Christian Books, 2d Series, No. 26). Association Press, 1959.

*Kee, Howard Clark, *Jesus and God's New People: The Four Gospels* (Westminster Guides to the Bible). The Westminster Press, 1959.

*Reicke, Bo I., *The Gospel of Luke,* tr. by Ross MacKenzie. Chime Paperback. John Knox Press, 1964.

Rollins, Wayne G., *The Gospels: Portraits of Christ*. The Westminster Press, 1964.

Stonehouse, Ned B., *The Witness of Luke to Christ*. Wm. B. Eerdmans Publishing Company, 1951.

THEOLOGICAL WORDBOOKS

*Allmen, Jean Jacques von, *A Companion to the Bible*, tr. from the 2d French ed. of *Vocabulaire Biblique* (1956), by P. J. Allcock, *et al.* Oxford University Press, 1958.

*Richardson, Alan, *A Theological Word Book of the Bible*. Macmillan Paperbacks 111. The Macmillan Company, 1962. First issued in 1950.

*Suitable for group Bible study in the local church.

III · The Beatitudes in Luke:
Royal Proclamation in Salvation
History

BLESSED ARE YOU POOR

BY WAY OF CONTRAST WITH MATTHEW, LUKE SPEAKS NOT OF
the poor in spirit but simply of the poor. As his usage
throughout makes clear (Luke 4:18; 7:22; 14:13, 21;
16:20, 22; 18:22; 19:8; 21:3), the poor are simply those
who have nothing. The poor, moreover, have a special
place in the whole of Luke's Gospel; and this is not because
of their poverty, as many have supposed, but because they
are the special object of God's grace. Jesus came to preach
to the poor (chs. 4:18; 7:22). It is to the poor that God
himself sends an invitation to sit at his banquet table in
his Kingdom (ch. 14:13, 21).

Along with the destitute, those without food or shelter,
Luke has tender concern for the unwanted and the dis-
inherited. Although in this respect he follows the course
taken by Mark (chs. 2:13-17; 10:17-31; 12:41-44) and Matthew (ch. 21:28-32), it is also true that he goes far beyond
them. Even the contrast that Luke draws between the rich
and the poor is more deeply etched (chs. 12:13-34;
16:19-31). According to Luke, Jesus himself belongs with
those prophets whom the Jews had rejected (ch. 4:20-30).
According to Luke, Jesus himself had a consuming love for
publicans and sinners and Samaritans (chs. 9:51-56;
10:29-37; 15:1-32; 17:11-19; 18:9-14; 19:1-10), men whose
very place in society put them beyond the pale of respect-

ability. In Luke's pages the very women whom Oriental custom put last now walk in the vanguard of Jesus' disciples (chs. 7:36-50; 8:1-3; 10:38-42). Indeed it is on this note that his whole Gospel begins (ch. 1:50-53). Luke 1:52, from the Magnificat of Mary, sounds the keynote of a moving symphony whose music we hear on every page: " He has put down the mighty from their thrones, and exalted those of low degree." It is just such folk who greet the birth of God's Son and who are on hand to receive his dying benediction (chs. 2:8-40; 23:39-43).

THE BEATITUDES AS PROCLAMATION

As witness to such grace so lavishly bestowed, the Beatitudes in Luke make Jesus' blessing a triumphant proclamation to the poor. Once again the contrast with Matthew is both obvious and striking. Matthew leans toward exhortation. Those whom he addresses are urged by implication to be poor in spirit, to hunger and thirst after righteousness, to be merciful and meek. Although the Jesus of Matthew does proclaim such people " blessed " and does so with Messianic authority, his majestic words are limited to the disciples he exhorts. On the contrary, the Jesus whom Luke depicts majors not in exhortation but in proclamation. The people whom he addresses are simply described as they are. Except in the fourth Beatitude, on persecution, nothing is expected of them. They are blessed not because of what they will do as disciples but because of the place where they stand. Jesus' blessing tells us less about them than about God's initiative toward them. They hunger. They weep. They are poor. They are hated. They are the downtrodden, the disadvantaged, the dispossessed. Because they have thus come to the end of their tether, God delights to lift them up.

THE BEATITUDES AS PROCLAMATION TO ALL ISRAEL

Luke now moves below the surface in two directions in order to emphasize that this proclamation is intended not for a small group of privileged disciples but for all Israel.

Although it is even difficult to determine the audience of Matthew's sermon, in Luke's case we are confronted by an extraordinary network of conflicting motifs. As with Matthew, both disciples and nondisciples are present (Matt. 5:1; 7:28; Luke 6:19-20; 7:1). But Luke's pointed address to the poor, the hungry, and the sad plunges us abruptly into uncharted depths. How far does he intend to go? His words of blessing are directed not to the virtuous but to the needy, and they are followed by four scathing woes. " But woe to you that are rich, for you have received your consolation. Woe to you that are full now, for you shall hunger. Woe to you that laugh now, for you shall mourn and weep. Woe to you, when all men speak well of you, for so their fathers did to the false prophets." It is difficult to imagine what place such woes have in an address to disciples! Quite clearly those addressed are not distinguished by their discipleship but only by the affluence they enjoy in wealth and social status. Moreover, such folk are worlds removed from the disciples so obviously laid under obligation in the immediately succeeding verse (Luke 6:27) : " But I say to you that hear, Love your enemies, do good to those who hate you." Just from such surface indications we must conclude that the Beatitudes and Woes of Luke are in fact a proclamation to the whole of Israel. To good and bad alike, to committed and uncommitted alike, they bear a common message about God. Because he is both sovereign and merciful he will turn the conditions of this world upside down.

Beyond this, Luke goes out of his way to put Jesus in precisely that place where such a general proclamation would be most appropriate. This is a fact which also lies below the surface, despite its tremendous importance. We can tell by following the two sections preceding his version of the Beatitudes that Luke at this stage uses Mark as his model. Luke 6:12-19 is quite clearly patterned on Mark 3:17-19 (paragraphs 71-72 of *Gospel Parallels*). However, as *Gospel Parallels* also shows, *Luke reverses Mark's order.* Mark first pictures Jesus ministering by the sea to a great multitude of people who press so hard upon him that to save his life his disciples must remove him to a boat offshore (Mark 3:7-12). It is only then that he goes into the hills to pray and to call to himself those who will be his most intimate followers (Mark 3:13-19). For both Mark and Matthew the mountain is the place to which Jesus calls his disciples to give them direction. *But Luke has it the other way around.* According to Luke, Jesus first calls his disciples in the mountain and then descends for his sermon to " a level place." Here we find along with the inner circle and a " great crowd " of disciples many other people as well. Luke not only adds woes to Beatitudes and phrases both in the most all-inclusive way, but he provides to hear them " a great multitude of people from all Judea and Jerusalem and the seacoast of Tyre and Sidon " (Luke 6:17). Jesus had withdrawn to the mountain, the traditional place of revelation, to name his twelve " apostles," but now he puts himself deliberately in a place more appropriate to the great proclamation he is about to make. " And he came down with them and stood on a level place. . . . And all the crowd sought to touch him, for power came forth from him and healed them all." (Ch. 6:17a, 19.)

PROCLAMATION AND SALVATION HISTORY: THE PURPOSE OF LUKE-ACTS

That the Beatitudes depict Jesus as the proclaimer of God's will is no happenstance. This function on Jesus' part is the central activity around which Luke gathers the main bulk of his narrative. Even more crucial is the place Luke gives to his story of Jesus. It is not an end in itself but the keystone of Luke's arch. Luke writes with the broadest possible perspective to show how God carries out his work of salvation through three separate periods of history. The middle period — as we have said, the keystone of Luke's arch — is the story of Jesus. Preceding it is the period of Israel, brought to focus in the ministry of John the Baptist; and following it is the period of the church, elucidated by Luke in the book of The Acts.

The period of Israel is rather sharply distinguished from that of Jesus at Luke 16:16: " The law and the prophets were until John; since then the good news of the kingdom of God is preached, and every one enters it violently." As with Q (Luke 7:18-35 and Matt. 11:2-19), Mark (ch. 1:1-3), and Matthew (chs. 3:2; 17:13), Luke contrasts Jesus and John; but unlike them he reserves the preaching of the gospel in a definitive way solely for Jesus (cf. Luke 3:18 and ch. 4:18-22). At the same time the experiences of John establish a pattern similar to that of Jesus. Both are born in difficult situations by the power of God (Luke 1:5-25, 26-38) for the salvation of God's people (vs. 46-55, 68-79). Like Jesus, but prior to his ministry, John is found both teaching (Luke 3:10-14) and preaching (vs. 3, 7-9, 18). Even his imprisonment is uniquely recorded by Luke prior to Jesus' baptism as if to provide in embryo a foretaste of Jesus' final fate (chs. 4:24; 13:33). Luke's point is twofold: not only is the God of the Law and the Prophets at work in the Baptist, but the pattern of his activity binds the period of Israel to that of Jesus. Although there is a break between John and Jesus, there is no break in God's power to effect his will through them.

The period of Jesus emphasizes his function as the proclaimer of God's Word. The key incident expressing this major motif is Jesus' visit to the synagogue at Nazareth,

a passage peculiar to Luke both in content and context
(ch. 4:16-30). Here he preaches authoritatively and pub-
licly as the anointed servant of Isaiah, specifically to the
poor (vs. 16-21). Here he takes his place as a rejected
prophet along with those servants of God whom Israel
had persecuted in the past (vs. 22-30). Here are fore-
shadowed even the universal thrust of his mission (vs.
25-27) and his final triumph over death (vs. 28-30). It is
this picture which Luke means to underline when he has
Jesus say, " I must preach the good news of the kingdom
of God to the other cities also; for I was sent for this purpose " (vs. 42-43). This is what lies behind the elaborate
setting Luke gives to his Sermon on the Plain (ch. 6:12-19)
as well as those summaries of Jesus' ministry found at chs.
7:22-23; 8:1; and 16:16. This motif reappears in the sending of the Twelve (ch. 9:2, 6), Jesus' feeding of the five
thousand (v. 11), and his first exhortation to discipleship
on the road to Jerusalem (v. 60). Public proclamation of
the Kingdom is the basic goal that motivates Jesus' whole
journey toward Jerusalem (chs. 11:20; 13:18-21; 14:15-24;
17:20-21; 19:11) and it is isolated for special emphasis at
its outset in the sending of the Seventy (ch. 10:8-11).
When this journey finally reaches its climax in the resurrection, the last glimpse Luke gives us of Jesus presents
him in the same light. Down to the very end he continues
to proclaim God's purpose as this is revealed in the events
whose form he himself determines (Luke 24:44-49; Acts
1:1-11).

When Jesus asks his church to proclaim his resurrection
(Luke 24:48), *the period of the church* begins. In Matthew
the risen Jesus simply recommissions the Twelve for their
new mission to the Gentiles (cf. Matt. 10:5-8; 28:16-20).
By thus stressing the continuity between Jesus' work before and after his resurrection, Matthew reaffirms his oft-
repeated equation of Kingdom and church. Luke is more

exact. He shows how a new historical epoch develops from the old, continuing the old but altering its pattern. By virtue of the new possibilities opened up by the resurrection, Jesus ceases his proclamation of the Kingdom and gives to the proclamation of the church an entirely new goal. Luke writes The Acts to follow the church in her expanding task. To allow for its completion, he postpones the Parousia in his reediting of Mark. This new mission must go on " until the times of the Gentiles are fulfilled " (Luke 21:20-24). Until then, the disciples, like Jesus, must preach the gospel with patience under persecution (chs. 21:12-19; 22:35-38; 24:44-48; Acts, chs. 3; 4; 5; 7; 10; 13; 14).

PROCLAMATION AND THE STRUCTURE OF LUKE'S GOSPEL

When Jesus proclaims the Kingdom, this both typifies and prepares the way for the proclamation of the church. Luke so structures his Gospel as to magnify this relationship. By describing the pilgrimage of Jesus from Galilee to Jerusalem he previews the later pilgrimage of the church from Jerusalem to the ends of the earth (Acts 1:8). By having Jesus commission two groups of disciples (Luke 9:1-6; 10:1-16) he sets the pattern of multiple mission so characteristic of The Acts (chs. 8:1-40; 10:1 to 11:26). Matthew works topically from discourse to discourse to prove that Jesus is indeed God's agent for salvation. Luke's narrative goes from event to event, through suffering to glory, to show how this salvation was realized in history (Luke 9:51; 13:33; 24:26).

The *prologue* (Luke 1:1 to 2:52) tells us that the life of Jesus was formed by that same sovereign grace he is called to proclaim. It brings before us a stately procession of humble folk whose paeans of praise announce what good things God has in store for all men.

Section I (chs. 3:1 to 9:17) pictures *Jesus in Galilee* in

the continuing act of proclamation to which our study of
the Beatitudes has already called attention. Following his
identification as God's Son (ch. 3:15-18, 21-22) in the context of world history (vs. 1-2) and Jewish history (vs.
23-38), he is brought to that special period of testing in
which his Sonship becomes unmistakably clear (ch.
4:1-13). It is then — at the threshold of his public ministry
— that Luke in his own special way presents Jesus as the
Servant-Messiah of Isaiah (vs. 14-30). The chapters that
follow picture Jesus fulfilling his mission in precisely this
role, always preaching and healing but always under threat
of rejection (chs. 4:36, 42-44; 5:15-17; 6:11; 7:1 to 8:3).
They also show his calling of the disciples and their initial
participation in that ultimate mission of proclamation
which awaits them as witnesses to his resurrection (chs.
5:1-11, 27-32; 6:12-49; 8:9-10; 9:1-17).

Section II (chs. 9:18 to 19:28) pictures *Jesus on his way
to Jerusalem*. Relying on much material that occurs only
in his Gospel, Luke uses this journey not with detailed
geographical precision but simply as a narrative framework
to indicate that Jesus is on the road toward Jerusalem (chs.
9:31, 51-53, 57; 10:1, 38; 13:22, 33-35; 17:11, 18:31; 19:1,
11). He goes to suffer so that through suffering he may be
glorified. The geographical motif is thus lifted up and
transformed into a theological motif. Jesus journeys to
that place where God's glory is to be supremely revealed
by his own resurrection and where consequently a major
turning point in the unfolding of God's purpose within
history is to be established. This motif is underlined in explicit terms. Suffering is clearly in store for both Jesus and
his disciples (chs. 9:21-22, 23-25, 43b-45, 53, 57-62;
12:49-56; 14:25-35; 18:31-34), often arising from the opposition of the Pharisees (chs. 11:14-23; 11:37 to 12:12;
16:14-15). As ch. 13:33 makes painfully lucid, Jerusalem is
the place of suffering: " Nevertheless I must go on my way
today and tomorrow and the day following; for it cannot

be that a prophet should perish away from Jerusalem."
At the same time it is made equally clear that Jerusalem
is the place where the glory of Jesus will be revealed. His
death is described as a new exodus in terms that recall the
experience of Moses (ch. 9:31), and this is followed by
the glory of the transfiguration (v. 32). At v. 51 the as-
cension of Jesus is clearly set forth as the goal of his
journey.

All the while Jesus continues his proclamation of God's
Kingdom and its coming (chs. 9:60; 10:9, 11; 12:31-32;
13:28-29; 14:15-24; 17:20-37; 18:16-17; 19:1-10, 11-27).
This includes another mission for the disciples, this time
involving seventy instead of twelve (ch. 10:1-24). In this
respect section II parallels section I and gives a foretaste of
what is to come as the church begins her proclamation on
the day of Pentecost.

Section III (chs. 19:28 to 24:53) ties up the narrative
threads we have been following as we see *Jesus in Jerusalem* to accomplish his mission there. Once more there is
prime emphasis on proclamation. In Luke alone Jesus is
hailed as King at his triumphal entry (ch. 19:38) and in
Luke alone his preaching and teaching during the last
week are confined to the Temple itself, presumably since
this is the place best suited for Israel to hear the proclamation of her King. His suffering is followed by the glory of
his resurrection, and this whole fulfillment is explained as
such in explicit terms (ch. 24:6-9, 25-27, 33-39). The glory
of the Parousia is postponed, perhaps to indicate that the
disciples, like their Lord, must endure suffering before
they can share his triumph (ch. 21:12-19, 34-36).

THE BEATITUDES IN THEIR "NATURAL HABITAT"
AS SALVATION HISTORY

When we move from one section to another of Luke's
Gospel we notice that the image of Jesus as the Anointed

Proclaimer of God's will, so brilliantly etched by the Beatitudes, is by no means lost. It is, rather, transformed and
amplified. In section II, Jesus continues to fulfill this role
on the road to Jerusalem by proclaiming the suffering and
the glory that awaits him there. Then in section III, when
the proclamation of section II has reached fulfillment, the
risen Christ continues his role as the proclaimer of God's
will by setting forth the next action that God will take in
the sending of his Spirit. Luke 24:44-49 should be read
again and again until its importance in this respect is
grasped. The image of Jesus is the same as in ch. 6:17-26,
but it has been transformed and amplified to suit the
change in circumstance effected by Jesus' resurrection and
death. Jesus is the Anointed Proclaimer still, just as he was
in pronouncing the Beatitudes. Now, however, his proclamation sets the stage not for his own resurrection triumph but for the proclamation of its consequence by the
church to the ends of the earth. With solemn dignity
Jesus gives marching orders for a new pilgrimage when
he says, " You are witnesses of these things " (ch. 24:48) .

If the Beatitudes thus bear the stamp of Luke's broad
purpose in the writing of Luke-Acts and take their place
in his Gospel by virtue of this fact, this is where our interpretation of them must begin. In the immediate fore-
ground we still see the towering figure of Jesus announc-
ing God's blessing upon the poor and his scathing, swift
judgment upon the proud. But when we understand that
Jesus does so as the Servant of Isaiah and that it is through
him that God is revealing a new stage in the development
of his promise, our attention is drawn beyond Jesus himself to the ultimate purpose that his proclamation serves.
As the history of the Baptist looks forward to Jesus' history, so his proclamation is a foretaste of what God will
accomplish through the church. It is God whose power
will reverse the lot of the poor and whose purpose will be
served by so doing and whose Spirit has anointed Jesus

to publish abroad these very tidings. We then understand that in Luke's story God himself is the major participant and the Beatitudes belong not simply to Jesus but to him. By revealing the pattern of God's saving activity in this world they become a major landmark in salvation history.

Such considerations help us to understand why Luke's blessing is so unconditionally given and his curse is so final and all-inclusive. Now it is no longer necessary for us to define the exact promise Jesus holds out to the down-trodden or what specific curse he calls down upon the haughty. Indeed it is better that we do not even try. For by the very context of his whole work Luke commends these words to us not so much as a specific message delivered by Jesus on a particular occasion, but, rather, as the kind of blessing and curse that must repeatedly fulfill itself whenever God visits his people. It is enough for us to reflect that, according to Luke, this is the Word which God sent to prepare his people Israel for the death and resurrection of his Son. The Beatitudes in *this* context, as vehicles of that Word, do not spell out the response true disciples should make, as they did in Matthew. As typical salvation history, they limit themselves simply to its proclamation.

ANOTHER POSTSCRIPT FOR THE INTERPRETER

Now that both Matthew and Luke have had their say, we seem to be as far as ever from answering our three unanswered questions. Matthew directs his Beatitudes only to disciples, whereas Luke insists that they be proclaimed to all Israel. Since such sharp differences lie deeply rooted in the structure of each Gospel, it would seem more difficult than ever to get back to Jesus. Knowing how basically they differ, we cannot treat either Gospel simply as a steno-graphic record. What the Evangelists have written is interpreted history. Although neither interpretation can be equated with the teaching of Jesus, one cannot be shunted aside in favor of the other. What shall we do?

Although we cannot get back to Jesus except by the witness of the Evangelists, we may not be as poorly off as it seems if we agree to recognize their witness for what it is — not stenographic reporting but authentic interpretation! We may take heart in having described this witness as fully as we have. With each Gospel's special bent in mind we should be in a better position to detect by contrast the primary intention of Jesus. Luke himself is our tutor here. Under the impact of the resurrection he does not hesitate to separate his own situation quite objectively from that of Jesus. If we consult the raw materials with which the Evangelists worked, perhaps we may understand their situation more thoroughly. Their interpretation is not necessarily a misinterpretation! Their interpretation properly used may bring us some solid answers after all! To test this faith, we shall attempt to explore the raw materials, both Christian and Jewish, in the next two chapters.

IV · The Raw Materials from the Christian Tradition

MANY READERS MAY FIND IT EASIER TO BEGIN WITH THE MORE general postscript at the end of this chapter, concerning the use of oral tradition by the church. Others will want to plunge immediately into the raw materials that lie just below the surface of the chosen passage in Matthew.

THE BEATITUDES IN MATTHEW'S SPECIAL MATERIAL (SOMETIMES CALLED " M ")

By using the comparative chart from Chapter I, we find that Matthew has five Beatitudes that do not appear elsewhere. If we extend the comparison begun there, we find that these Beatitudes are only the first of five blocks of material that either occur only in Matthew or exhibit interests we have found characteristic of him. Following the Beatitudes we come upon:

A. Matt. 5:13-14, " You are the salt of the earth; but if salt has lost its taste, how shall its saltness be restored? . . . You are the light of the world. A city set on a hill cannot be hid." These are discipleship sayings with a typical Matthean flavor.

B. Matt. 5:17-20, four verses affirming the supremacy of the law and the necessity of fulfilling its demands, concluding with, " For I tell you, unless your righteousness exceeds that of the scribes and Pharisees, you will never enter the kingdom of heaven."

C. Matt. 5:21-48, six antithetic propositions setting Jesus' word over against the law, where the antithetic pattern seems to originate with Matthew, "You have heard that it was said to the men of old, . . . but I say to you." One such antithesis does occur at Luke 6:27, but there it is probably due to Luke himself, so that the pattern of comparison between Jesus' word and the law here emerges as an interest characteristic of Matthew's special material. Here it affects murder, adultery, divorce, oaths, retaliation, and the love of one's enemies.

D. Matt. 6:1-18, where this antithetic pattern is extended to cover the traditional Pharisaic pillars of piety, alms, prayer, and fasting. "And when you pray," says Jesus in typical Matthean idiom, "you must not be like the hypocrites," that is, the Pharisees.

The underlying motif in all these verses is the same. Although the worth of the Old Testament is affirmed, its basic purpose is seen to be fulfilled by both Jesus and his disciples, as over against the Pharisees. When we ask why material thus unified in content should be so compactly ordered and occur in such a continuous sequence, the only answer seems to be that it belonged originally to a collection of the oral teachings of Jesus that was made prior to the writing of the present Gospel. We have discovered one of the sources with which the Evangelist worked, one major item among the raw materials upon which he drew.

Before the Evangelist wrote what we now know as the Sermon on the Mount he probably had an embryo "sermon" in this special source of his, headed by the five Beatitudes we isolated in Chapter I. If this is true, then his own arranging of the Sermon on the Mount to form the first great discourse of his Gospel was not entirely new. He simply amplified what he found in his raw materials. Long before the first Evangelist set to work, a preceding generation of Christian believers knew Jesus as exalted Lord and arranged his teachings to exhibit this judgment by setting at the beginning a collection of his own special blessings.

THE BEATITUDES IN Q, THE MATERIAL AVAILABLE TO BOTH MATTHEW AND LUKE

This same pattern emerges when we compare the whole of Luke's Sermon on the Plain with Matthew's Sermon on the Mount. To carry out this comparison in detail it is best to observe paragraphs 18-44 side by side with paragraphs 73-78 of *Gospel Parallels*. Since it is impossible to reduplicate as much material as this in these pages, we print below, for those who do not have access to it, some excerpts from the Index of *Gospel Parallels* that will form the basis of the observations we now wish to make about the two major Sermons.

Before using this Index, we remind ourselves of the comparative columns from *Gospel Parallels* printed in full at the outset of the first chapter. There we saw that four of the Beatitudes ascribed to Jesus occur in both Matthew and Luke. Though phrased in the sharply different forms that we have already observed, they deal successively with Jesus' blessing on the poor, the hungry, the sorrowing, and the persecuted. The assumption usually made concerning these four Beatitudes is that they belonged to a source held in common by both Matthew and Luke and as such circulated in the oral tradition prior to their incorporation in our present Gospels. In themselves, then, they are another item from the raw materials with which the Evangelists worked. We have made a second significant " find " by digging below the surface.

As with the special material of Matthew, so also with Q, the Beatitudes occur in the context of a whole Q " sermon." It is this that comes to light by observing the relevant material in *Gospel Parallels,* or by using the following items from its Index:

THE SERMON ON THE PLAIN — Luke 6:20-49

Paragraph No.	Content	Luke	Parallels from Matthew
73	The Beatitudes	6:20-23	*5:3, 4, 6, 11, 12*
74	The Woes	6:24-26	No parallel
75	On Love of One's Enemies	6:27-36	*5:39-42, 44-48; 7:12*
76	On Judging	6:37-42	*7:1-5;* 10:24-25; 15:14
77	A Test of Goodness	6:43-46	*7:16-21;* 12:33-35
78	Hearers and Doers of the Word	6:47-49	*7:24-27*
79	The Centurion's Slave	7:1-10	*7:28a;* 8:5-13

On the basis of the comparisons tabulated in this Index we may make the following observations:

1. The whole of Luke's Sermon is reproduced in Matthew's Sermon except for the Woes of Luke 6:24-26.
2. The *sequence* in which the Q material common to both Sermons occurs is *exactly the same* in both Gospels, except for one major realignment represented by Matt. 7:12 (and two lesser changes at ch. 5:4 and vs. 44-46). This major realignment as well as the continuity in sequence may be observed by following the italicized passages from Matthew's Sermon in the fourth column.
3. Each Sermon begins with Beatitudes and ends with the same parable. The very next block of material each Gospel shares with the other following this parable is also the same — namely, the story of the centurion's slave.

It should now be obvious that there were not only Beatitudes in the source shared by Matthew and Luke but also a complete " sermon " in itself, beginning with these same four Beatitudes and ending with the same parable.

It is also highly probable that this Q "sermon" is reproduced by Luke at ch. 6:20-49. With the exception of the Woes, Matthew reproduces *all* the material in Luke and arranges this material in *exactly the same sequence.* Why does he do this? Probably because he had before him, as one of his major sources, a "sermon" that read very much like what we now observe in Luke 6:20-49. Surely we may list this as a third significant "find" in our digging. We need only pick up the sixth chapter of the Gospel of Luke and read what is said there from verses 20 to 49 in order to have before us (with the exception of the Woes) what almost certainly existed in much this form as a major source among the raw materials used by both Evangelists prior to the writing of the present Gospels. With the help of Luke we have penetrated to the pre-Gospel period.

THE BEATITUDES IN MATTHEW'S SERMON ON THE MOUNT

We may take time at this point to reflect for a moment on what Matthew did with the sources at his disposal. Although the conclusion we are ready to draw is obvious, we must state it deliberately and keep it steadily in mind during the whole of our subsequent study.

Both the Sermon on the Mount, Matt. 5:1 to 7:28, and the Beatitudes that stand at its beginning, Matt. 5:3-12, are the composition of the first Evangelist. Although he did not create the raw materials we have isolated from the pre-Gospel period, he did put them in their present form. If we are to interpret his interpretation of Jesus in the proper way, this is what we must remember at every step. The Evangelist wove together from Q and M both their Beatitudes and their "sermons" in order to complete in his own way what had been begun by those who transmitted these raw materials to him.

The Beatitude on Persecution

When we observe that this is the only Beatitude which appears quite clearly in Matthew, Luke, M, and Q, we have ample reason to separate it from all the rest for special consideration.

In the material peculiar to Matthew, the M form of this Beatitude may well appear at Matt. 5:10. It is here stated in the third person and promises blessing upon all those persecuted for the sake of righteousness. In Q (Matt. 5:11-12 and Luke 6:22-23), this Beatitude is stated more directly in the second person and puts major emphasis on those persecuted for the sake of Jesus himself. Matthew has obviously combined the two versions by setting them down side by side, whereas Luke has apparently reworked what he derived from Q.

In both what we can reconstruct of M and Q and what we now find in Matthew and Luke, this Beatitude is longer than any of the others. More than the others it participates quite broadly in the experience of the early church. We hear in it the familiar overtones of persecution (as in Mark 13:9-13) combined with apocalyptic expectation (as in Luke 17:22-37). More broadly still we find other forms of this Beatitude in both I Peter and James, ministering there to Christians in suffering by holding out the hope of eternal reward and exhorting to joy. I Peter 3:14 reads, " But even if you do suffer for righteousness' sake, you will be blessed." In a similar vein, I Peter 4:12-14 carries this exhortation: " Beloved, do not be surprised at the fiery ordeal which comes upon you to prove you, as though something strange were happening to you. But rejoice in so far as you share Christ's sufferings, that you may also rejoice and be glad when his glory is revealed. If you are reproached for the name of Christ, you are blessed because the spirit of glory and of God rests upon you." Similar words appear at James 1:12, " Blessed is the man who endures trial, for when he has stood the test he will receive the crown of life which God has promised to those who love him."

What does it mean that blessing, persecution, and joy are thus joined in so many different forms and appear in so many different sources? At the very least we may conclude that this Beatitude was transmitted independently before it found its place in M and Q.

THE WOES OF LUKE

A somewhat more difficult problem presents itself in the Woes of Luke 6:24-26. Were they known also to Matthew but omitted by him in this place so that he could use them more effectively in ch. 23? Or were they not known to Matthew, not part of the Q source he shared with Luke, and consequently do they owe their place in this part of the tradition to Luke alone? We favor this latter solution, though the data are not clear enough to affirm it with absolute certainty.

The facts are these. No one can deny that Luke's Woes were formulated to match the complete roster of his Beatitudes. They are four in number, occur in the same order, and employ many of the same terms, even down to the word " now " that gives so sharp an eschatological contrast to the second and third items in each listing. Moreover, if Luke's first Beatitude (by way of comparison with Matthew's) sets us to wondering whether the " poor " are spiritually sensitive or sociologically depressed, the added Woes take away every doubt. They are in fact a materialistic reinterpretation of the preceding Beatitudes. This is generally recognized by all scholars today.

Although all such facts point to the hand of Luke, two further considerations seem to blur this impression. Although Luke's Woes are patterned for the most part on his own Beatitudes, three of them evidence a possible con-

nection also with the Beatitudes of Matthew. The relevant
items appear as follows:

Matthew	*Luke*
Blessed are those who *mourn,* for they shall be *comforted.*	Woe to you that laugh now, for you shall *mourn* and weep.
Blessed are you *when men . . . utter all kinds of evil against you.*	But woe to you that are rich, for you have received your *consolation.*
	Woe to you, *when all men speak well of you.*

This comparison might suggest that Luke's Woes were
first formulated in a stage preceding the construction of
his Gospel with materials influenced by either M or Matthew. To add to this observation, we must recall that the
first words of Luke 6:27, " But I say to you that hear,"
represent a quite definite attempt on Luke's part to bridge
the gap between his last Woe and the vigorous exhortation
to discipleship that follows immediately upon it. If Luke
himself were so conscious of this pronounced break in his
material that he went out of his way to mend it, how can
we attribute to him the very woes that intensify the differences he works so hard to overcome?

I think we may do justice to these perplexing data by
making the following proposal. If we assume that Luke did
indeed put his Woes in their present form, we may also
assume that the materials he used were not created by him,
but were taken from a common tradition, reflections of
which appear also in Matthew. The words for " mourn "
and " comfort " or " consolation " probably stem from Isa.
61:1-2, a passage frequently drawn upon to interpret the
life of Jesus. If the final Beatitude on persecution occurs in
so many different forms and sources, we need not be surprised to find that Luke's corresponding Woe reflects what
appears also in Matthew.

Beyond all such negative considerations, we may see in Luke's creation of these Woes a quite positive religious motive. If he saw in the Beatitudes of Q the element of eschatological proclamation that shines through his rendering of them, he may well have set down the corresponding Woes in order to underline just this note. We may freely admit then that he understood both Beatitudes and Woes in a physical sense as over against the obvious spiritualizing of Matthew. But we must also remember at the same time that his basic interest was not moral or sociological but eschatological. Luke would then have used the Woes to publicize beyond all shadow of doubt the radicality of Jesus' announcement of blessing. Beatitudes and Woes taken together fairly shout aloud that the new age of God's great upheaval has come.

Having arranged his material to highlight such a message, Luke may well have taken special pains to separate this eschatological promise from the ethical demand that follows in v. 27. This desire to distinguish promise from demand would account for his elaborately constructed phrase of transition, " But I say to you that hear." Moreover, he would not have hesitated to join such seemingly discordant materials since both would represent, though in different ways, the radicality of God's inbreaking reign. On the one hand, the Beatitudes and Woes extend in a radical way the gift God is now making to men, with the consequences of its rejection plainly spelled out. On the other hand, the radical demand for obedience would spell out with equal clarity what the coming of God's Kingdom might really mean for those who had accepted this gift. Luke's contribution (as over against Matthew's) would be to separate grace from demand or Gospel from Law, thus making clear that the initiative and the gift are in God's keeping, not ours. No longer may we pretend, as by a superficial reading of Matthew, that blessing is conditional upon obedience. According to Luke, whether men respond or not, God's gift of himself is as free and universal as his sovereign power and infinite mercy.

THE BEATITUDES AND JESUS

We should stop to remind ourselves that such conclusions as we have been drawing must be given due weight in our interpretation of Jesus. For example, we can no longer rely on the composite Beatitudes of Matthew for a faithful presentation of Jesus' total message in this respect, simply because they are, in their present form, the work of the Evangelist and not of Jesus himself. Again, we must give priority in our interpretation to those Beatitudes shared by both Evangelists — the Beatitudes of Q — and put much greater emphasis than has heretofore been put on Luke's eschatological understanding of them. In addition we may postulate a different context in the ministry of Jesus for the Beatitude on persecution than for the others and we need not feel bound to attribute the Woes in their present form and context to our Lord himself.

A POSTSCRIPT ON THE ORAL TRADITION

When we talk about the raw materials that circulated in the pre-Gospel period, we must be at some pains to make one fact about them very clear indeed. Although the conclusions we have drawn about the nature and extent of these materials must be acknowledged as tentative, the fact of their existence can be solidly established. Of this there can be no doubt whatsoever.

Take, for example, two of our earliest witnesses, Luke and Paul. Luke, in writing his two books, speaks of material " delivered to us by those who from the beginning were eyewitnesses and ministers of the word " (Luke 1:1-4). Paul also speaks of what he had " delivered " to the Corinthian church about the Last Supper (I Cor. 11:23-26) and the resurrection (I Cor. 15:3-7). The word " deliver " itself is a technical term taken from Judaism where it was used to indicate what the Jewish rabbis handed down orally to their successors.

Paul seems to be following some such official tradition when he discusses with the Corinthians the question of divorce. At one point, he has a definite word from the Lord, " To the married I give charge, not I but the Lord, that the wife should not separate from her husband " (I Cor. 7:10). When he goes on to discuss marriage between believers and unbelievers he has no specific bit of tradition from the words of Jesus and says so: " To the rest I say, not the Lord, that if any brother has a wife who is an unbeliever, and she consents to live with him, he should not divorce her " (v. 12). So also we find Paul quoting from his fund of Jesus' words one Beatitude that did not secure a place in the Gospel canon. Our informant is Luke at Acts 20:35: " In all things I have shown you that by so toiling one must help the weak, remembering the words of the Lord Jesus, how he said, ' It is more blessed to give than to receive.' "

In the second place, we must keep in mind the double perspective that always attends each word of Jesus in the tradition. As we saw in Chapter II, what the earliest Christians preserved of Jesus' teaching tells us as much about them as about him. As we maintained in closing Chapter III, the " situation-in-life " of the church must be carefully delineated and held in tension with that of Jesus. Only so can both *Sitz-im-Leben* be properly understood and the words of Jesus be properly interpreted.

Consider, for example, Paul's admonition to the Corinthians about divorce, referred to above (I Cor. 7:10-16). When we ask what light Paul throws on the words of Jesus, it is important both to evaluate the conflict of believer with unbeliever in Corinth's pagan culture and to notice that Paul agrees with Mark's interpretation of Jesus over against that of Matthew. Whereas Matthew allows one legitimate reason for divorce, Mark and Paul allow none (Mark 10:1-12; Matt. 19:1-12; 5:32). What has influenced this outcome? Was Jesus himself more strict or more lenient? Are we listening to him, or to the rabbinic viewpoint of Matthew in the struggle of church and synagogue, or to the clash of Christian and pagan standards amid the complexities of cosmopolitan Hellenistic culture? In order to gain an answer to such questions we must go even farther afield than we have to probe in depth at least the Jewish environment in which Jesus first spoke his Beatitudes and the church first mediated them to the world. This we shall do in the next chapter.

Meanwhile we should call attention to the two disciplines that have been most influential in modern times in promoting the kind of analysis on which this chapter has been based. They are source criticism and form criticism. The first studies the oral tradition at the relatively late point in its development where it has jelled into easily identifiable collections of Jesus' words and deeds. In the process of describing these sources, modern scholars have concluded that Matthew and Luke were written after Mark, that each drew on both Mark and Q, and that each had in addition a special body of material not available to the other (sometimes denoted by the letters *M* and *L*).

Form criticism identifies the more plastic literary forms in which the oral tradition was first transmitted, such as the parables or the miracle stories. It then attempts to write a history of the typical development of each form from simple to complex or from early to late. The German word, *Formgeschichte,* or " form history," is still the best description of this endeavor.

The bibliography that follows should open up these disciplines to those who may have some inclination to expore them further. It first lists some standard works related to each discipline and then recommends some treatments of Matthew's Sermon in which the application of source criticism and form criticism may be traced with profit from the beginning of the century to the present.

BIBLIOGRAPHY

SOURCE CRITICISM AND FORM CRITICISM

Bornkamm, Günther, *et al.*, *Tradition and Interpretation in Matthew*, tr. by Percy Scott (The New Testament Library). The Westminster Press, 1963. Mature, provocative.

Bultmann, Rudolf, *The History of the Synoptic Tradition*, tr. by John Marsh. Harper & Row, Publishers, Inc., 1963. A classic in its field.

———— " A New Approach to the Synoptic Problem," *Existence and Faith: The Shorter Writings of Rudolf Bultmann*, sel., tr., and intro. by Schubert Ogden. Living Age Books, No. 29. Meridian Books, Inc., 1960.

———— and Kundsin, Karl, *Form Criticism: Two Essays on New Testament Research,* tr. by Frederick C. Grant. Harper Torchbooks, TB 96. Harper & Row, Publishers, Inc., 1962. Basic essays, first issued in 1934.

Dibelius, Martin, *From Tradition to Gospel*. Charles Scribner's Sons, 1935. A pioneer study by a recognized master in this field now available in paperback (SL124).

———— *The Message of Jesus Christ: The Tradition of the Early Christian Communities,* tr. by Frederick C. Grant. Charles Scribner's Sons, 1939. Lucid and interesting guide for beginners.

Easton, B. S., *The Gospel Before the Gospels*. Charles Scribner's Sons, 1928. Original, provocative treatment by a veteran scholar.

Fuller, Reginald, *Interpreting the Miracles*. The Westminster Press, 1963. Excellent use of critical method, easily digested.

Grant, Frederick C., *The Gospels: Their Origin and Growth*. Harper & Brothers, 1957. Superb analysis.

Guy, Harold A., *A Critical Introduction to the Gospels*. London: Macmillan & Co., Ltd., 1955. Best survey to begin study of the Synoptics.

Jeremias, Joachim, *The Parables of Jesus,* 6th ed., revised, tr. by S. H. Hooke. Charles Scribner's Sons, 1963. Most valuable form-critical treatment of the parables.

Lightfoot, R. H., *History and Interpretation in the Gospels.* Harper & Brothers, 1935.

McGinley, Laurence J., *Form-Criticism of the Synoptic Healing Narratives: A Study in the Theories of Martin Dibelius and Rudolf Bultmann.* Woodstock College Press, 1944.

Moule, C. F. D., *The Birth of the New Testament* (Harper's New Testament Commentaries). Harper & Row, Publishers, Inc., 1962. Form-critical survey of entire field; mature, imaginative, highly readable.

Redlich, Basil, *Form Criticism: Its Value and Limitations.* London: Gerald Duckworth & Co., Ltd., 1948.

Riddle, Donald W., *The Gospels: Their Origin and Growth.* The University of Chicago Press, 1939. Radical.

Riesenfeld, Harald, *The Gospel Tradition and Its Beginnings: A Study in the Limits of " Formgeschichte."* London: Canterbury Press, 1961.

Taylor, Vincent, *The Formation of the Gospel Tradition.* London: Macmillan & Co., Ltd., 1933. Best reappraisal of Bultmann and Dibelius. By veteran scholar, seasoned in Gospel research.

—— *The Gospels: A Short Introduction.* London: The Epworth Press, 1946.

STUDIES IN THE SERMON ON THE MOUNT *

Bacon, B. W., *The Sermon on the Mount: Its Literary Structure and Didactic Purpose.* The Macmillan Company, 1902.

Dupont, J., *Les Béatitudes. Le Problème littéraire. Les Deux Versions du sermon sur la montagne et des béatitudes.* Nouvelle édition. Bruges: Abbaye de Saint-André, 1958.

Grayston, K., "Sermon on the Mount," *The Interpreter's Dictionary of the Bible,* ed. by George Buttrick, Vol. R-Z,

*Consult also the books by Windisch, Dibelius, and Jeremias from the bibliography of Chapter I. For its analysis of both the underlying sources and the individual sayings, the study by Jeremias is an excellent place to begin one's reading.

pp. 279–289. Abingdon Press, 1962.

Manson, T. W., *The Sayings of Jesus as Recorded in the Gospels According to St. Matthew and St. Luke.* London: SCM Press, Ltd., 1949. A reprint from *The Mission and Message of Jesus,* 1937, by Major, Manson, and Wright. Landmark in source criticism by a pioneer. Invaluable.

Marriott, H., *The Sermon on the Mount.* London: S.P.C.K., 1925.

Votaw, Clyde W., " Sermon on the Mount," *A Dictionary of the Bible,* ed. by James Hastings. Charles Scribner's Sons, 1905. Extra Volume, pp. 1–45.

Wilder, Amos N., " The Sermon on the Mount," *The Interpreter's Bible,* Vol. 7, pp. 155–164. Abingdon Press, 1951.

V · The Raw Materials from Contemporary Judaism

WORDS, WORDS, WORDS

WE WHO LIVE IN THE '60'S OF THIS CENTURY KNOW WHAT A bewildering shower of new words has accompanied the many changes our common life has undergone. One need only close his eyes and think for a moment of " TV," " H-bomb," " astronaut," " radar," " jet stream," " computer," or " Iron Curtain "! Never before has history unleashed so many new words in so short a time.

We should not, then, be surprised to find that the words of the ancient Biblical text were given their first meanings by the history that spawned them. Nor should we wonder if these ancient words do not have the same meaning for us as they had for those who used them so long ago. Even our more recent past should alert us to the changes that time can make in word usage. " Blackguard " once meant, not a scoundrel, but a cleaner of sooty pots. A " crafty " fellow once described an artisan skilled at some craft rather than one who lives by stealth. In John Wycliffe's translation of the New Testament, Christ advises the rich young ruler to come and " sue " him, since " sue " in the fourteenth century meant simply to " follow " and not (as it does for us) to initiate proceedings in a court of law.

If we are to do justice to such words as " blessing," " poor," " kingdom," " righteousness," " mourn," " comfort," " peacemaker," or " prophet," we must carry farther the word study begun in Chapter II. Just to illustrate what needs to be done, we may inquire about the history or the " situation-in-life " of the word " poor." What meanings did it have before it was incorporated into the two versions of the first Beatitude? As it stands there we may think of its designating either material poverty or spiritual receptivity. Blessing falls either upon the destitute (Luke) or upon those whose spirit is humble (Matthew). Which meaning did Jesus intend? Would it help us to decide if we had better knowledge of the word " poor " as used in his environment?

The Poor in the Old Testament

Although there are several Hebrew words that are translated by the word " poor " in the RSV Old Testament, the one of most importance for us conveys, by its very root, much more than material poverty. It points basically to someone who has been ill-treated, a person made miserable by some kind of misfortune. Such misfortune may indeed be material poverty in any one instance, but the word just as often brings to the fore a whole host of other factors, as in Isa. 3:14-15, where the poor are the victims of social oppression.

Beyond the root meaning of this one Hebrew word — when all the related roots are considered and their varied contexts weighed — we come upon a far-reaching and vigorous theology of " social action." The poor are the special concern of God. Since the land belongs to him and the nation owes its very existence to him, it is his will that none should perish from want. This concern appears very early in Hebrew history. A Hebrew slave must be set free after six years (Ex. 21:2). Every seventh year the land must lie fallow " that the poor of your people may eat " (ch. 23:11). In dispensing justice (v. 6) or lending money (ch. 22:25) or arranging sacrificial offerings (Lev. 5:7), the

poor must be given preferential treatment. Such concern
is restated by the Deuteronomic code in the most emphatic
way. " But there will be no poor among you (for the Lord
will bless you in the land which the Lord your God gives
you for an inheritance to possess), if only you will obey
the voice of the Lord your God, being careful to do all this
commandment which I command you this day." (Deut.
15:4-5; cf. chs. 15:7-18; 24:10-14, 17-18.) It is on this basis
that the prophets protest when the privileged take ad-
vantage of the underprivileged. " ' What do you mean by
crushing my people, by grinding the face of the poor? '
says the Lord God of Hosts." (Isa. 3:15.) It is from this
perspective that these men of God again and again speak
for him against injustice (Isa. 5:8; 10:1-4; Amos 2:6-7;
4:1-3; 5:11). In his name they promise retribution for the
oppressors (Amos 2:9-16; 8:1-14; Micah 2:1-3; Isa. 1:21-31;
Ezek. 22:23-31), and help for the oppressed (Isa. 14:32;
25:4; 26:5-6; 29:17-21; Jer. 20:13; Zeph. 3:11-13). So it is
in the exile, when his people are " afflicted " and " poor,"
that God puts himself on their side (Isa. 41:17-20; 49:13;
51:12-16; 54:11; 61:1-3).

Only when we understand the totality and depth of
God's concern for the poor as this is set forth in the Law
and the Prophets can we appreciate their situation as de-
picted in the psalms. The " poor " of the psalms are most
often seen facing their oppressors and calling upon God
for deliverance. " For the needy shall not always be for-
gotten, and the hope of the poor shall not perish for ever.
Arise, O Lord! Let not man prevail; let the nations be
judged before thee! " (Ps. 9:18-19.) The first and last
verses of Ps. 10 are typical. " Why dost thou stand afar off,
O Lord? Why dost thou hide thyself in times of trouble?
In arrogance the wicked hotly pursue the poor; let them
be caught in the schemes which they have devised. . . . O
Lord, thou wilt hear the desire of the meek; thou wilt
strengthen their heart, thou wilt incline thy ear to do jus-

tice to the fatherless and the oppressed, so that man who is
of the earth may strike terror no more." (Ps. 10:1-2, 17-18.)
It is the business of the king to help the poor (Ps. 72:1-4,
12-14), as it is God's will to rescue them (Ps. 69:30-33;
82:1-4; 94:1-23).

It should be easy now to see what has happened to the
word " poor." The poor are not simply destitute but oppressed. The poor not only may expect God's help as their
due, but characteristically are found calling upon him
with the overwhelming confidence that he will hear them.
As the poor range themselves on God's side, they thus appear to be men of faith and righteousness. Although the
word " poor " has not lost its material sense, it has taken
on quite definite overtones of a spiritual and religious
kind. The poor and the righteous stand in the same place
(Ps. 14:4-6; 34:1-6, 15-19; 140:12-13; 146:5-9). They cry
to God for deliverance (Ps. 12; 18; 22; 40:13-17; 74:18-23;
86).

If we now ask what help the Old Testament gives us in
solving the problem posed by the Beatitudes, we cannot
return a simple answer. On one level, to be sure, we may
affirm with certainty that the word " poor " in itself often
goes far beyond material want. On another level, however,
the very question with which we began loses its original
urgency because the focus of our interest has shifted from
man to God. The Old Testament challenges us not simply
to ask in what sense a man is poor in the circumstances of
his daily existence, but in what relation a " poor " man
stands to God for the granting of existence itself. If we
follow this lead, we can only define poverty in terms of a
man's total involvement in the whole of creation. The
creature in all the weakness and agony of his creaturehood
stands naked before the mercy of the one who created him
and who wishes to redeem him.

From the Old Testament to the New

If words change their meaning, taking on new lights and shades as they are used in new circumstances, we cannot afford to move directly from the Old Testament to the New. As we know with increasing certainty, Jewish religious life in the Hellenistic period (from 200 B.C. to A.D. 100) was highly complex. There were many points of view expressed in a great variety of ways which a rich literature has preserved for us in considerable quantity. We know enough to characterize rather sharply at least five separate groupings: the Pharisees, the Sadducees, the Essenes, the Zealots, and the Samaritans. The literature remaining to us includes at least the Apocrypha, the Pseudepigrapha, the Dead Sea Scrolls, and the Mishnah, not to mention the works of Philo and Josephus.

The Apocrypha comprises some fifteen separate writings lying outside the Hebrew canon but included in the ancient Greek and Latin Bibles of the Christian church. The word "apocryphal" stems from a Greek root meaning "to hide." Although we commonly think of what is apocryphal as being "false," the word as used here does not have that meaning. It refers simply to what lies outside a specific official canon. (Such books would be "hidden" probably in the sense given that word by ch. 14 of II Esdras, where Ezra is commanded to write ninety-four books in all but is allowed to publish only twenty-four. The remaining seventy must be kept hidden, that is, their message made available only to the wise.) Some of these works were written to supplement the Old Testament, such as the interesting story of Bel and the Dragon, whose hero is Daniel. Others, like I Maccabees, are historical accounts and still others, like Tobit, are fiction intended to glorify Jewish virtue. II Esdras is an apocalypse. The two most influential writings — The Wisdom of Jesus the Son of Sirach and The Wisdom of Solomon — are akin to such canonical Wisdom literature as Proverbs or Ecclesiastes.

In addition to the officially recognized Apocrypha which may now be bought as part of the RSV Bible, there are other " outside " books not so well recognized or named and not so widely available. They are usually called " Pseudepigrapha," since they are falsely ascribed to such ancient Old Testament heroes as Moses, Enoch, or Abraham. For the most part they are strongly " apocalyptic." The word " apocalyptic " is derived from a Greek root meaning " to reveal." Apocalyptic writings propose to divide history into predetermined periods whose end will be marked by an obvious revelation of divine power, resulting in the judgment of the wicked and the rewarding of the righteous. They " reveal " the various schematic patterns of historical development by which their authors suppose that the end will come. Such pseudepigrapha as I Enoch were popular among the Essenes of the Qumran community near the Dead Sea, since their whole outlook on life was apocalyptic to the core. They felt, for example, that history would end in a Messianic conflict of forty years' duration and they had organized their members to participate in it as " sons of light " for the final victory over Satan. We cannot enter into larger detail here, but full descriptions of the Apocrypha and the Pseudepigrapha and the Dead Sea Scrolls may be had in the works listed at the end of this chapter.

The same is true of rabbinic literature. This literature consists of commentary on the Old Testament by the rabbis as passed on orally from the earliest times. It is cumulative, since each generation of rabbis comments not only on the Old Testament but also on what their predecessors had said about it. According to a commonly accepted pattern, such commentary would be either Halakah, the formulation of rules and definitions, or Haggada, nonjuristic teaching of a moral, religious, and more homiletical nature. The earliest formal collection of such material in

written form (made around A.D. 200) was the Mishnah and
this was followed (up to A.D. 500) by many other writings,
notably by the Palestinian Talmud and the Babylonian
Talmud.

THE POOR APART FROM QUMRAN

If we exclude for the moment the Dead Sea Scrolls, what
picture do we have of the " poor " in the literature we
have just described? Although we have space only to tabu-
late our results in a somewhat mechanical way, the study
of this literature brings great rewards. By comparing how
it differs from or agrees with both the Old Testament and
the New, we may discover in a tentative way what was of
most importance for the contemporaries of Jesus.

1. It cannot be stressed too heavily that there was a continuing emphasis on charity. As we have it from Prov.
14:31, " He who oppresses a poor man insults his Maker,
but he who is kind to the needy honors him." The same
counsel is given at Sirach 4:1-10 and is reiterated constantly
by the rabbis. When Tobit sends his son Tobias on his
journey, it is just this advice he gives to him: " Do not turn
your face away from any poor man, and the face of God
will not be turned away from you " (Tobit 4:7b) .

2. We must also take notice of a contrary trend. Sometimes the bitter results of poverty are simply described
without relating the poor to God, " A man honored in
poverty, how much more in wealth! And a man dishonored
in wealth, how much more in poverty! " (Sirach 10:31) .
At Sirach 40:28, a commendable sympathy is expressed for
the lot of the poor: " My son, do not lead the life of a beggar; it is better to die than to beg." At the same time, riches
are praised (Sirach 40:18) , poverty is attributed to indo-
lence (Prov. 6:6-11) , and charity is recommended only
when extended to the upright (Sirach 12:4-5) . " Give to
the godly man, but do not help the sinner."

3. A third trend may be observed that carries farther the sharp division noted in the canonical psalms between the poor and their oppressors. Many scholars feel that " the poor " spoken of there constituted a specific " party " of men who looked upon themselves as righteous over against the wicked and the rich. As George Foot Moore puts it: " The distinctive thing in this outcry is that the social strife deepens into a religious cleavage. The poor and humble are in their own consciousness the pious; they denounce their adversaries as ungodly. The ill-treatment they suffer is conceived as persecution for righteousness' sake." [1] Reflections of such a sharp social division are evident in The Wisdom of Solomon 2:10-20, Sirach 13:3-7, 15-23, in three of the Psalms of Solomon (5; 10; 15) , and particularly at I Enoch, chs. 94-104. In I Enoch, the antagonism between rich and poor takes on an eschatological coloring with the pronouncement of repeated woes on the rich at the Final Judgment (I Enoch 96:1-8) . It is not surprising that I Enoch enjoyed currency among the Essenes at Qumran or that some scholars now wish to attribute to them the Psalms of Solomon, for it is certainly in an eschatological context that the " poor " appear in the Dead Sea Scrolls.

THE POOR AT QUMRAN

As almost everyone knows by this time, the first of the Dead Sea Scrolls turned up in 1947 in some elongated jars embedded in the floor of a cave. This cave, later known as Cave I, opened on the face of a high limestone cliff overlooking the northwestern shore of the Dead Sea. Below the high cliffs of Cave I lies a great marl terrace, and below this terrace, or plateau, lies the Maritime Plain that borders the Dead Sea. Cutting through cliff and terrace to the Maritime Plain runs a dry riverbed known as the Wadi Qumran. Near that point where the Wadi Qumran cuts a deep gorge to the Dead Sea, but high above it on the marl terrace or plateau, lies an ancient *khirbeh*, or " ruin," suspended, as it were, between cliff and plain. This ruin archaeologists have positively identified as the wilderness retreat known from ancient sources to have been built in this vicinity by the Essenes.

Apparently from the second century B.C. almost to the destruction of Jerusalem in A.D. 70, Khirbet Qumran was a nerve center of Essene activity. Eleven caves have now been uncovered in this vicinity yielding their treasured manuscripts. For some two miles both north and south, there is evidence that the devotees of this sect lived in caves or tents or huts, with Khirbet Qumran as their community center. Here they stored water, prepared food, and made pottery; they buried their dead nearby. But above all, it was here that they carried out their cultic practices and copied and read their precious manuscripts, both Biblical and non-Biblical.

Of most importance for us are the following, each designated in a triple way. The number indicates the cave in which the particular work was found, the letter *Q* stands for Qumran, and the final letter refers to each document's Hebrew title describing its contents.

1. The Manual of Discipline or Community Rule (1QS).
2. The War Rule or The War of the Sons of Light and the Sons of Darkness (1QM).
3. The Book of Hymns or Psalms of Thanksgiving (1QH).
4. The Damascus Document or the Zadokite Document. A copy of this was first found many years ago in Cairo. (*CD*)
5. Various commentaries on books of the Bible. The two of interest to us are the Commentary on Habakkuk (1QpHab.) and that on Psalm 37 (4QpPs. 37). The *p* in each case stands for the Hebrew word *pesher*, meaning roughly " explanation."

The Essenes from Qumran thrived on their own specific eschatological interpretation of the Old Testament. Dissatisfied with the corruption of the Temple hierarchy, they separated themselves from it and at one point in their history went into the Judean wilderness around the Dead Sea to prepare there — quite literally according to Isa. 40:3-5 — for the coming judgment of God. They lived by a strict moral and ritual code, exacting a more meticulous discipline from their members than the Pharisees would ever have dreamed of imposing. By following this communal rule, they hoped to prepare themselves for the manifestation of God's anointed leader in the last days. He would appear in their midst and lead them to victory over Satan in a grueling forty years' war, the war of the sons of light against the sons of darkness.

Now it is just these people who used hymns comparable to the Old Testament Psalter in which they saw themselves as the persecuted " poor " of the Psalter tradition. If we use the excellent translations of *The Essene Writings from Qumran* by A. Dupont-Sommer, we can examine in detail (column and verse) the passages in which they refer to themselves specifically as " the poor ": 1QH 1:36; 2:32, 34; 3:25; 5:13-22; 18:14-15. Just how official this term was as a self-designation of the sect is sharply debated, but there can be no doubt that the Essenes interpreted their whole existence as the life of God's poor, under persecution by his enemies until the coming of the final age would secure their release. It had been so at the beginning when the Wicked Priest persecuted their forebears (1QpHab. 12:3, 6, 10) . They know themselves as " the Congregation of the Poor " still under duress (4QpPs. 37 2:10) . But they look forward to the final days when, as " the poor whom Thou hast redeemed," they may fight with God against their enemies to gain ultimate and complete victory (1QM 11:9-13; 14:7) . A typical expression of their viewpoint comes at 1QH 5:20-22.

I give Thee thanks, O Adonai,
for Thou hast not abandoned the orphan
nor despised the needy!
for Thy might is (fathomless)
and Thy glory immense,
and wonderful Valiant Ones are thy ministers.
And (Thou hast) set my foot in the sweepings,
    in the midst of the humble,
in the midst of them that are quick unto
    righteousness,
to cause all the poor of Grace
to arise from the tumult together.

QUMRAN AND THE BEATITUDES

Apart from this general application of the word " poor,"
we find at 1QM 14:7 the specific phrase "the humble in
spirit." Since this phrase affords an exact parallel in the
Hebrew to the Greek of Matt. 5:3, scholars have gone to
great lengths to determine its meaning, hoping that in
this respect Qumran might throw direct light on the Gospel of Matthew or even upon the actual words of Jesus.
Professor Kurt Schubert, of the University of Vienna,
would translate this phrase " voluntarily poor " [2] in order
to stress the fact that the Essenes voluntarily gave up their
material goods to the common treasury, and despised
riches. Père Simon Legasse, of France, starts from the word
" spirit " as indicating that inward perfection of spirit with
which the Essenes accepted persecution.[3] A third view also
begins with the word " spirit " but takes it to mean " Holy
Spirit," the Spirit of God rather than a spirit within man.
Because they were endowed with the Holy Spirit, the Essenes thought of themselves as distinct from all others.
They used the phrase " poor in spirit " in order to express
this conviction.[4]

The proponent of this third view, Prof. David Flusser,
of the Hebrew University of Jerusalem, would go even far-

ther in making claims for the Beatitudes of Matt. 5:3-5. He finds an exact parallel to all three Matthean Beatitudes at 1QH 18:14-15. In this hymn, the Teacher of Righteousness, the founder of the Essene sect, speaks of his mission. Following Isa. 61:1-2 and drawing upon ch. 66:2, he is to preach good news to " the humble " and to console " the contrite of spirit and the afflicted," precisely the folk addressed in Matt. 5:3-5. According to Professor Flusser, Matt. 5:3-5 thus shows that Jesus also spoke with the same authority and to the same people as the Teacher of Righteousness. This is to say that Jesus was conscious of the Essene ideal and addressed himself to those who held it dear. This correspondence in words and audience, according to Professor Flusser, would give obvious priority to the Matthean form of the Beatitudes over the Lucan.

Working from a different passage (4QpPs. 37), Prof. Frank Cross, of Harvard, finds in the Qumran interpretation of Ps. 37 an anticipation of Luke 6:20-21.[5] The Essenes at Qumran say not only that they are " the Congregation of the Poor " who shall triumph in the Last Day, but that they will eat then at God's great eschatological banquet on the high mountain of Israel, thus recalling Luke 6:21a: " Blessed are you that hunger now, for you shall be satisfied."

THE OLD TESTAMENT, QUMRAN, AND JESUS

By way of conclusion we may sum up the impact of Qumran and the Old Testament on our interpretation of Jesus.

A. With the challenge of Professor Flusser before us we must ask quite earnestly whether we can in fact give preference to exact words used by either Matthew or Luke. This is a larger subject than the data collected in this one chapter would suggest, so that we can only indicate some tentative conclusions in brief.

1. It is probable that the Beatitudes were originally cast in a poetic form, and this is usually interpreted to favor Matthew. The claim is made that if the Greek of Matthew is retranslated into Aramaic, some sort of Aramaic poetry emerges that may then be regarded as the basic text for determining the words of Jesus. However, one of the most recent and thorough attempts to do this must draw on both Gospels in order to establish a poetic pattern and does not succeed in penetrating beyond such a pattern to establish specific words.[6]

2. It still can be conjectured with a high degree of probability that behind the present Greek texts lay some sort of Aramaic original. Some of the differences between the Greek of Matthew and that of Luke may be explained as translation variants. What we find in the Greek arose as different translators understood the Aramaic words and idioms in contrary fashion. It is by such reasoning that Jeremias accounts for the differences between Matt. 5:12 and Luke 6:23.[7] It has also been shown that the Greek word for "satisfied" (upon which Matt. 5:6 and Luke 6:21 agree) is paralleled by an Aramaic word meaning "stall-fed," and that in the rabbinic literature this word is applied as in Matthew to God's feeding of the righteous.[8] However, all such reconstructions are perilous, and even if they were not, we could not assume *ipso facto* that the Aramaic of the tradition was necessarily that of Jesus.

3. Whenever specific words are weighed against each other to isolate what Jesus may have used as over against the tradition, one must always keep in mind the particular bias of each Evangelist. But even when this is done the result is uncertain. If "poor in spirit" fits Matthew's narrower discipleship context, the simple word "poor" also fits the wide-ranging interests of Luke. If "righteousness" is a favorite with Matthew, it also occurs in other forms of the Beatitudes outside the Gospels (I Peter 3:14). If the word "mourn" in Matt. 5:4 depends on Isa. 61:2 or

" meek " in Matt. 5:5 depends on Ps. 37, it still cannot be determined whether the use of these passages originated with Jesus or is the result of that rabbinic exegesis which so often appears in the Gospel of Matthew (ch. 13:52).

4. We must exercise similar caution when called on to evaluate the Qumran material discussed above. None of this material seems sufficiently compelling to require our assigning to Jesus either the Matthean or the Lucan version of the Beatitudes. Too many questions remain unanswered. Since the midrashic exegesis that combined Isa., ch. 61, with Ps. 37 was open not only to Jesus and the men of Qumran but also to Matthew, it is impossible to tell on this basis alone with which of the three the particular combination of Matt. 5:3-5 originated. Once more, how does it happen that Matthew combines Isa., ch. 61, with Ps. 37, whereas the Qumran exegetes treat the latter separately and appeal also to Isa. 66:2?

B. If the materials thus far discussed are not closely enough related to enable us to establish the exact words of Jesus, there can be no denying that Jesus and Qumran both draw upon the same general fund of religious experience, so that comparisons between them should prove fruitful in other areas. To this we now turn.

1. Although every member of the Qumran community was required to put his property at the disposal of his brethren, and the community did draw upon a common store of food and water, the word " poor " does not seem to have been particularly associated with this practice.[9] Moreover, although this practice expresses a common concern for the physical welfare of the whole community, we do not find in it any more than a pale reflection — if indeed that — of the vigorous protection offered by God in the Old Testament to the least and poorest of his people. Although the Covenanters of Qumran bound themselves to fulfill the law of love to its utmost (CD 6:14–7:6), they seem to stop in their concern at the boundary line of their

own cult. By way of contrast we are compelled to ask whether the attitude of Jesus is not much broader, less exclusive, and a good deal more vigorous than this. In all our sources, but particularly in Luke, he appears to take special pains to extend the promise of the Kingdom to those in greatest need, no matter what their other qualifications or lack of them might be. Here Jesus and the men of Qumran move in opposite directions. Jesus seems to have caught more fully than they the Old Testament's robust concern for the whole of Israel.

2. On the other hand, for both Jesus and the men of Qumran, the word " poor " surely had taken on spiritual and religious connotations. Nor can we deny to either one the same passionate concern for the vindication of God's poor that is echoed in the canonical Psalms. If we take Luke's version of the Beatitudes in the fullness of its basic thrust, we can feel in it the pulsebeat of the Psalmist's cry just as we sense this in the Qumran Psalms of Thanksgiving. For both, the needy and the righteous stand in the same place before God. Whether Jesus is here responding directly to Qumran or making his own independent interpretation of the Old Testament is not clear, but this fact must not obscure for us the basic likeness in their approach. Both Jesus and the men of Qumran know the Lord God of Israel as the one who vindicates his own.

3. In still one further area the men of Qumran travel considerably beyond the Old Testament and by so doing, provide us with a valuable criterion for our understanding of Jesus. Whereas in the Old Testament Psalter we find a vigorous hope that God will finally rescue the oppressed among his people, in the Scrolls this hope is brought to a well-defined apocalyptic focus. Jewish apocalypticism usually describes the last days in terms of a cosmic struggle between God and Satan, a struggle we find at Qumran in their War Rule. Likewise Jewish apocalyptic works also emphasize the great gulf that looms between the age in which

their authors live and the final time when all the ills they suffer will be done away by the consummation of this cosmic struggle. Whereas nothing of this sort appears in the canonical Psalter, it is just such an apocalyptic framework as this that the Scrolls use to make their presentation of " the poor."

The Essene elect speak of " the time of wickedness " (*CD* 6:14), when they live in lowliness and distress, under persecution by their enemies (1QH 5:13-19). By way of contrast they hope for " the time of good-will " established by God when " the just " will possess " eternal salvation and perpetual unfailing peace " (1QH 15:15-16). It is just such an apocalyptic eschatology that they have in mind when the men of Qumran identify themselves as " the Poor of Grace," those who are poor now but who in the future will be lifted up from their poverty by the grace of God. They will " arise from the tumult together " (1QH 5:22). When they speak of themselves as " the Poor whom Thou hast redeemed," they recall their lowly estate but look forward to the time when, as those redeemed by God, they will assist him in the overthrow of Satan (1QM 11:9). The same is true when the Qumran elect picture themselves as " the humble in spirit." Although we cannot erase from this celebrated phrase the connotations proposed for it by Schubert, Legasse, and Flusser, the actual context in which it occurs opens up quite another dimension. At 1QM 14:7 the " humble in spirit " are those whose oppressed state will be reversed by God when they participate with him in his final victory over " all the wicked nations." Both here and elsewhere the word " poor " appears as a kind of technical term within the Qumran vocabulary. Its meaning has been stereotyped to express the very special apocalyptic expectations entertained by the sect. By emphasizing the lowliness of God's beloved elect, it acts as a foil to affirm their coming vindication in the Messianic Age.

This tension between present and future, between hu-

miliation and exaltation, is nowhere more emphatically
described than by the Qumran *pesher* on Ps. 37. Verse by
verse the " secrets " of this psalm are " explained " by their
application to the Essene sectarians. Verse 11 of the canonical psalm promises that the meek shall inherit the earth.
For the Qumran commentator this means that the Qumran "poor " will be delivered in " the time of affliction "
preceding the end (4QpPs. 37 1:9). Verses 21-22 of the
canonical psalm renew the promise of v. 11, and from this
the Qumran sectarians conclude that they as " the Congregation of the Poor . . . will possess the sublime Mountain
of Isra(el and) will taste (everlasting) delights (in) His
holiness " (4 QpPs. 37 2:10-11). This eschatological interpretation is probably derived from the promises of Ezek.
17: 23; 20:40; and 34:14. It expresses the conviction that
the men of Qumran, although persecuted now, will one
day be gathered as the flock of God and fed by him on his
holy mountain.

Such an apocalyptic interpretation of " the poor " at
Qumran poses the question of how far we are justified in
setting the teaching of Jesus in a similar framework.

By relating the blessing of Jesus to the Kingdom, the Beatitudes in both Matthew and Luke do give to Jesus' message an eschatological focus. " Eschatology " stems from the
Greek root *eschatos,* meaning " last." Assuming that God
brings his plans to a final fruition, eschatology describes either the " last times " or the " last events " preceding it.
Often in Jewish thought the Kingdom appears in some
such context as a future good to be brought about by the
fulfillment of all God's promises. Thus the Beatitudes affirm that with the coming of God's Kingdom the poor will
be blessed, the merciful shown mercy, the sorrowing comforted, and the hungry fed.

Thus far the Beatitudes travel with Qumran beyond the
Old Testament. The question we must now ask in the next
chapter is how far this agreement persists. Does the ten-

sion set up by the Beatitudes between the present and the future also involve a cosmic struggle between God and Satan and a fixed distinction between an age of sorrow and one of bliss? In other words, is the eschatology of Jesus apocalyptic in nature? If so, how far does it agree or disagree with the apocalypticism peculiar to the Dead Sea Scrolls?

NOTES

1. George F. Moore, *Judaism in the First Centuries of the Christian Era* (Harvard University Press, 1927), II, p. 156.

2. Kurt Schubert, "The Sermon on the Mount and the Qumran Texts," *The Scrolls and the New Testament,* ed. by Kristar Stendahl (Harper & Brothers, 1957), pp. 118–128. See also Kurt Schubert, *The Dead Sea Community,* tr. by John W. Doberstein (Harper & Brothers, 1959), pp. 85–88, 137–139.

3. Simon Legasse, "Les Pauvres en Esprit et les 'Voluntaires' de Qumran," *New Testament Studies,* VIII (July, 1962), pp. 336–344.

4. David Flusser, "Blessed Are the Poor in Spirit," *Israel Exploration Journal,* X (1960), pp. 1–13.

5. Frank M. Cross, Jr., *The Ancient Library of Qumran and Modern Biblical Studies* (Doubleday & Company, Inc., 1958), pp. 61–62, 67n81.

6. Matthew Black, *An Aramaic Approach to the Gospels and Acts,* 2d ed. (Oxford: Clarendon Press, 1954), pp. 258–260.

7. Joachim Jeremias, *The Sermon on the Mount* (Fortress Press, 1963), pp. 15–16.

8. Morton Smith, *Tannaitic Parallels to the Gospels* (Journal of Biblical Literature Monograph Series, Vol. VI, The Society of Biblical Literature, 1951), pp. 24–25.

9. A direct connection between word and practice is established by only one passage (4QpPs. 37 2:10) and that only in the unique translation given this passage by Theodore H. Gaster, *The Dead Sea Scriptures in English Translation* (Anchor Book, A 92; Doubleday & Company, Inc., 1956), pp. 260–261. "This refers to that congregation of poor men who (make over) their entire estate to the (common fund)."

BIBLIOGRAPHY

The Old Testament

Achtemeier, Paul and Elizabeth, *The Old Testament Roots of Our Faith.* Abingdon Press, 1962. Along with de Dietrich and Napier the best place to begin.

Anderson, B. W., *Understanding the Old Testament.* Prentice-Hall, Inc., 1957. Like Gottwald's, an easy to read, authoritative survey, putting Israel's literature and religion in its proper historical setting.

Bright, John, *A History of Israel.* The Westminster Press, 1959. Along with Eichrodt, von Rad, and Noth an indispensable guide for advanced students.

Dietrich, Suzanne de, *The Witnessing Community: The Biblical Record of God's Purpose.* The Westminster Press, 1958.

Eichrodt, Walther, *Theology of the Old Testament,* tr. by J. A. Baker. Vol. I. The Westminster Press, 1961.

Gottwald, N. K., *A Light to the Nations.* Harper & Brothers, 1959.

Napier, D., *Song of the Vineyard: A Theological Introduction to the Old Testament.* Harper & Row Publishers, Inc., 1962.

Noth, Martin, *The History of Israel.* London: Adam & Charles Black, Ltd., 1958.

von Rad, Gerhard, *Old Testament Theology.* Vol. I. Harper & Row, Publishers, Inc., 1962.

The Apocrypha and the Pseudepigrapha

Charles, R. H. (ed.), *The Apocrypha and Pseudepigrapha of the Old Testament.* 2 vols. Oxford: Clarendon Press, 1913.

Metzger, Bruce M., *An Introduction to the Apocrypha.* Oxford University Press, Inc., 1957.

Pfeiffer, R. H., " The Literature and Religion of the Apocrypha," " The Literature and Religion of the Pseudepigrapha," in *The Interpreter's Bible,* Vol. I (Abingdon Press, 1952), pp. 391–436.

Rowley, H. H., *The Relevance of Apocalyptic: A Study of Jewish and Christian Apocalypses from Daniel to the Rev-*

elation, rev. ed. Association Press, 1964.

*Russell, David S., *Between the Testaments.* Muhlenberg Press, 1960.

THE RABBINIC LITERATURE

*Baron, S. W., and Blau, J. L. (eds.), *Judaism: Postbiblical and Talmudic Period* (The Library of Liberal Arts). The Bobbs-Merrill Company, Inc., 1954. Selections translated.

Danby, Herbert (tr.), *The Mishnah.* Oxford: Clarendon Press, 1933. Basic text.

Daube, David, *The New Testament and Rabbinic Judaism.* London: The Athlone Press, 1956.

Montefiore, Claude J. G., and Loewe, H. M. J. (eds. and trs.), *A Rabbinic Anthology.* Meridian Books, JP 32. The World Publishing Company, 1963.

THE DEAD SEA SCROLLS

Burrows, Millar, *The Dead Sea Scrolls.* The Viking Press, Inc., 1955.

────── *More Light on the Dead Sea Scrolls.* The Viking Press, Inc., 1958.

Dupont-Sommer, André, *The Essene Writings from Qumran,* tr. by G. Vermes. Meridian Books, MG 44. The World Publishing Company, 1962. Translation, commentary.

*Fritsch, Charles, *The Qumran Community: Its History and Scrolls.* The Macmillan Company, 1956.

Gärtner, Bertil, *The Temple and the Community in Qumran and the New Testament.* Cambridge: Cambridge University Press, 1965.

Milik, Józef T., *Ten Years of Discovery in the Wilderness of Judaea,* tr. by J. Strugnell (Studies in Biblical Theology, No. 26). Alec R. Allenson, Inc., 1959.

*Ringgren, Helmer, *The Faith of Qumran: Theology of the Dead Sea Scrolls.* Fortress Press, 1963.

*Stauffer, Ethelbert, *Jesus an'd the Wilderness Community at Qumran.* Facet Books, Biblical Series, No. 10. Fortress Press, 1964.

*Books so listed are the best to begin on. To go farther with the Scrolls, consult Burrows, Milik, Dupont-Sommer, and Cross.

COMPREHENSIVE SURVEYS

Barrett, C. K. (ed.), *The New Testament Background: Selected Documents.* Harpertorch Books, TB 86. Harper & Brothers, 1961.

Bible Key Words, from Gerhard Kittel's *Theologisches Wörterbuch zum Neuen Testament.* Tr. and ed. by J. R. Coates. Harper & Brothers, 1951. This is the first of five volumes translating key items from Kittel, among them " righteousness " and " kingdom."

Davies, William D., *The Setting of the Sermon on the Mount.* Cambridge: Cambridge University Press, 1964. Monumental probing of the *Sitz-im-Leben.*

Driver, S. R., " Poor," *A Dictionary of the Bible,* ed. by James Hastings, Vol. IV, pp. 19–20. Charles Scribner's Sons, 1902.

Hastings, James (ed.), *A Dictionary of the Bible,* rev. ed. by Frederick C. Grant and H. H. Rowley. Charles Scribner's Sons, 1963.

The Interpreter's Dictionary of the Bible, ed. by George A. Buttrick. 4 vols. Abingdon Press, 1962. At present, the most comprehensive and up-to-date survey in English, for such terms as " Apocrypha," " apocalypticism," " Dead Sea Scrolls," " eschatology," " Essenes," " Hebrew religion," " Kingdom of God," " Messiah," " poor," " Beatitudes," " righteousness."

Kittel, Gerhard (ed.), *Theological Dictionary of the New Testament,* tr. and ed. by G. W. Bromiley. Wm. B. Eerdmans Publishing Company, 1964. Still in process. Aims to translate Kittel's superb volumes *in toto.*

Peake, A. S., *Commentary on the Bible,* rev. ed. by Matthew Black and H. H. Rowley. Thomas Nelson & Sons, 1962.

VI · The Beatitudes in the
Teaching of Jesus

THE KINGDOM OF GOD

THE BEATITUDES TAKE US DIRECTLY TO JESUS' TEACHING about the Kingdom of God. If we should study this phrase as we studied the word " poor," we should find that it refers basically to the rule that God exercises over his creation. Simply by virtue of his being a righteous and merciful creator, God's right to rule is unlimited. It is in these terms, for example, that he addresses the pagan King Cyrus: "I am the Lord, and there is no other, besides me there is no God " (Isa. 45:5). In spite of this inherent sovereignty, however, God's actual sovereignty over his creation is always limited by virtue of its continuing rebellion against him. The story of God and man in Hebrew thought is the story of God's attempt to establish in actual fact what belongs to him by inherent right. By the time of Jesus, Hebrew history had resolved this tension in two quite different ways. According to one view, the Kingdom might be realized when an individual agreed to submit his entire life to God's rule, when, for example, he took upon himself the yolk of the law. According to a second view, the Kingdom could only come in the future when God would take the initiative on his own to make his rule effective over the whole of his creation, whether or not mankind agreed. It is this latter view which we have already met at Qumran (1QM 6:6; 12:7). It is expressed quite well by

The Assumption of Moses 10:1 where the following is said of God,

> And then His kingdom shall appear
> throughout all His creation,
> And then Satan shall be no more,
> And sorrow shall depart with him.

It is just this view which we also meet in Jesus, although he introduces into it a startlingly new element. While he points to the time when God will rule completely, he also finds in his own ministry that this rule has already begun. The promise of future blessing is already finding fulfillment in the present. Although Jesus moves in the same direction as the Essene Covenanters, his thought creates its own special patterns. What the men of Qumran had reserved only for the future he finds happening now.

Jesus finds the proclamation of this message quite urgent, since what God is doing to establish his sovereignty among his people creates a genuine crisis. This is not simply (as we might suppose) a crisis of decision to test whether men will line up with Jesus or against him, although such decision is indeed called for. The crisis to which Jesus points lies much deeper than that. In Jesus' ministry, God now pours forth the fullness of his own life energy. So far as he can, he reestablishes the health and harmony he had intended for his whole creation at the start. The law is radically reinterpreted, massive forgiveness is offered, ancient hostilities are overcome, a new fellowship is born, the sick and the sick at heart alike are lifted up. God himself so enters into man's ancient struggle for salvation that the course of his history can never be the same again.

Beyond this upheaval Jesus sees another, a final, crisis when God will finish once and for all what he has now begun afresh. Thus the distinctive mark of Jesus' ministry is the tension it reflects between these two moments of crisis:

the one at whose storm center he himself and his disciples now stand and the other that will soon erupt for all mankind. The blessing he offers in itself lifts this tension to full view as it vibrates between the pull of both crises, the one already in effect and the other still to come. " Blessed are you that hunger now, for you shall be satisfied." (Luke 6:21.)

What we have outlined here by way of orientation we must now explore in detail.

THE CRISIS NOW: GOD OFFERS HIMSELF ANEW

That God willed to initiate a crisis among his people first becomes clear in his sending of John the Baptist (Acts 10:37; Mark 1:1-4) . All our records show that Jesus looked upon John as one sent from God. He praised him as " more than a prophet " (Luke 7:26) . He accepted John's baptism (Mark 1:9-11) . He defended his own authority by appealing to that of John (Mark 11:27-33) . He put his own rejection and that of John on the same footing. He and John would be justified by God, whereas those who rejected them would be condemned (Luke 7:31-35) . We even have from Jesus a quite sweeping word giving to John an absolutely crucial place in the coming of God's Kingdom. If we weigh the two forms given this word by Matthew and Luke (Matt. 11:12; Luke 16:16) , we can see that with John one era closed and another opened. " The law and the prophets were until John " (Luke 16:16a) , but " from the days of John the Baptist until now the kingdom of heaven has suffered violence " (Matt. 11:12a) .

If John had been sent by God, so also had Jesus. In one of his most pungent sayings he opens his mind to us without hesitation: " He who receives you receives me, and he who receives me receives him who sent me " (Matt. 10:40; compare Luke 10:16; Mark 9:37) . At the same time Jesus knew that his own work was quite different. With his ministry new powers had come into play that had not been given to John. This comes to the fore in two stylized accounts, each reflecting a special interpretation of his ministry by the Evangelists, but both very probably going back to Jesus himself through Isa., ch. 61. The first comes at Matt. 11:2-6. What we sense here is a tension between John and Jesus in their struggle to interpret God's will for his people. John had expected his ministry to end in a cataclysmic judgment (Matt. 3:10) and had undoubtedly assigned some part in it to Jesus (Matt. 3:11-12). But Jesus knew better. Jesus understood John better than John understood himself. Before the coming of judgment all the vitality of God's own life must be poured out among his people for their refreshment. It is in this light that we should interpret the words of Jesus recorded at Matt. 11:4-5: " Go and tell John what you hear and see: the blind receive their sight and the lame walk, lepers are cleansed and the deaf hear, and the dead are raised up, and the poor have good news preached to them. And blessed is he who takes no offense at me."

John was a voice crying in the wilderness, taking up in his own way the task that the Essene sectarians imposed upon themselves (Mark 1:3; Isa. 40:3; 1QS 8:12-16). If God had given to John the role of Elijah (Mark 9:12-13; 1:2; Mal. 3:1; 4:5-6), for Jesus he had reserved something quite different. It would be the task of Jesus to herald an era of mercy (Isa. 29:18-19; 35:5-6; 61:1-2a). This glad announcement appears also in the second of the two accounts stylized by Luke to throw Jesus' own countrymen at Nazareth in conflict with him (Luke 4:16-30). Over against their narrow nationalism Jesus throws open the gates of God's goodwill to all those whom they despised. So we read at Luke 4:18-19, " The Spirit of the Lord is upon me, because he has anointed me to preach good news to the poor. He has sent me to proclaim release to the captives and recovering of sight to the blind, to set at liberty those who are oppressed, to proclaim the acceptable year of the Lord." If the Teacher of Righteousness revered by the Essenes could formulate his mission in terms of Isa., ch. 61 (1QH 18:14-15), the use of this text by Jesus need not surprise us, particularly in the light of his subsequent ministry. Quite clearly Jesus believed that God was offering himself in new and fresh ways to his people and felt that he had been chosen to make this known.

Nowhere is this more evident than in the healing ministry of Jesus. Above all else, his healing is accomplished by the power of God's Spirit, and for Jesus this in itself is first-hand evidence that God has already begun to rule. " But if it is by the finger of God that I cast out demons, then the kingdom of God has come upon you." (Luke 11:20.) As the record of numerous healings shows (Luke 13:16; Mark 5:6-8), the exorcisms performed by Jesus are viewed as his victory over Satan. As Jesus explains it, " But no one can enter a strong man's house and plunder his goods, unless he first binds the strong man " (Mark 3:27). Since he has bound the strong man, Satan, he can speak of his ministry as a time of blessing sent from God. In this sense Jesus has already accomplished in part what the elect of Qumran could only hope for as the outcome of their forty years' war in the Messianic time. Only of that far future conflict could they affirm, " This shall be the time of salvation for the people of God, the hour of dominion for all the men of his lot and of final destruction for all the lot of Belial " (1QM 1:5). By way of sharp contrast we hear Jesus' glad cry of victory when the Seventy return from their mission. " The seventy returned with joy, saying, ' Lord, even the demons are subject to us in your name! ' And he said to them, ' I saw Satan fall like lightning from heaven.' . . . Then turning to the disciples he said privately, ' Blessed are the eyes which see what you see! For I tell you that many prophets and kings desired to see what you see, and did not see it, and to hear what you hear, and did not hear it.' " (Luke 10:17-18, 23-24.)

Perhaps the loveliest sign of newness in Jesus' ministry is his overwhelming sense of God's forgiving love. Without hesitation he pronounces sins forgiven (Mark 2:5; Luke 7:47-50) and instructs his disciples to ask for such forgiveness daily, using the most intimate terms in their address to God (Matt. 6:9, 12). It is just here that the power of God's new approach to Israel shines most brightly. The disciples are able to forgive each other — even to seventy times seven — only because they can be certain that God has forgiven them (Luke 17:3-4; Matt. 18:21-22). The two parts of the petition for forgiveness are inseparable: " And forgive us our debts, As we also have forgiven our debtors " (Matt. 6:12). This is not a calculated attempt to bargain with God, but the simple recognition that God's goodness to us is the source of our power to forgive each other.

It is in this way that God creates around Jesus a new society. For not only do Jesus' disciples know themselves forgiven and not only can they forgive each other, but this same power is, first of all, resident in him. It is Jesus' own deep reliance on God that secures for him such enormous capacity to forgive others, both his enemies and the outcasts whom they have dispossessed. There was a dictum in Jesus' society that put such publicans as Levi and Zacchaeus beyond the pale. Yet it is just these men to whom Jesus throws open the gates of the Kingdom without reserve (Mark 2:13-17; Luke 19:1-10). None were more hated than the Samaritans, and yet it is just these men whom Jesus singles out for special attention (Luke 9:51-56; 10:29-37; 17:11-19).

As we learn many times in the Gospels, this new company of disciples whom God chose to gather about Jesus became a threat to the established order. Over against that order the marvel of Jesus' ministry is this: that instead of withdrawing from the conflict that inevitably ensued he threw these same powers of forgiveness in the direction of his enemies. Instead of withdrawing from the keepers of Israel's law and cult as had the men of Qumran, he laid siege to their hearts with all the strength at his command. Again and again he tried to draw them out of the pit they had dug for themselves. He spoke to them of the good Samaritan, the forgiving father, the lost sheep, the lost coin, the laborers in the vineyard, and the unforgiving servant, beseeching them to forgive as they had been forgiven (Luke 10:29-37; 15:1-32; Matt. 18:23-35; 20:1-16). And at the end this was his final legacy to those who put him to death. " Father," he cried, " forgive them; for they know not what they do." (Luke 23:34.)

The contrast with the men of Qumran at this juncture is enormous, even when all allowances have been made to see them in the best possible light. There is no denying that the Qumran Covenanters also had a deep sense of God's love for them. As their hymns testify, they constantly gave thanks for his help to them and particularly for the knowledge he had revealed for their guidance (1QH 11). What stronger proof of this do we need than the hymn that closes the Manual of Discipline (1QS 11:2-22)? Its deep faith in God's forgiving grace matches the best in Christian piety. " He has justified me by His true justice and by His immense goodness He will pardon all my iniquities " (1QS 11:14). Even when they think of evil men, the elect of Qumran know that they should do them good. " To no man will I render the reward of evil, with goodness will I pursue each one; for judgment of all the living is with God, and He it is who will pay to each man his reward " (1QS 10:17-18). At the same time, their drive for perfection and their very insistence upon God's righteousness separated the Essene sectarians from their enemies while it engendered an eagerness to see them punished. If we read just a few lines farther on in the Manual, this is what we find: " As for the multitude of the men of the Pit, I will not lay hands on them till the Day of Vengeance; but I will not withdraw my anger far from perverse men, I will not be content till He begins the Judgment. I will be without malice and wrath towards those that are converted from rebellion but merciless to those that have turned aside from the way " (1QS 10:19-21).

If such contrasts with Qumran bring us closer to the grace that God had bestowed on Jesus, they also help us to understand his Beatitudes. It is no accident that in pointing to the newness of his mission or in pointing to his exorcisms as God's victory over Satan, Jesus also pronounces a blessing upon his hearers (Matt. 11:6; Luke 10:23). The very fact that God is imparting his life anew through Jesus in itself creates the conditions in which such blessing is appropriate. " Blessed are the eyes which see what you see! For I tell you that many prophets and kings desired to see what you see, and did not see it, and to hear what you hear, and did not hear it." The same is true of Jesus' power to forgive and the new life it engenders in Israel. Since God has so acted, the time is ripe to herald his blessing abroad. His deed and his word, eschatological presence and Beatitude, go hand in hand.

When Jesus thus stands as God's emissary to pronounce his word of blessing, we know once and for all that God is again visiting his ancient people and that we can be glad about it. We know this from both Matthew and Luke since in both such glorious promises are held forth with such unmistakable authority. But we know it particularly from Luke since in his form of the Beatitudes the initiative of God in the giving of himself is so obvious. For Luke, God's blessing depends not on moral virtue but simply on human need. For Luke, God's blessing reaches not simply a consecrated few but the whole of the created universe to uproot and overturn all injustice. The hungry shall be fed and the sorrowing made glad because God wills it so. Many times Jesus had imparted this glad message to his hearers in the familiar parables of growth. In spite of obstacles, he had assured them, God is indeed at work and will certainly bring his harvest to its appointed fruition. What he accomplishes will not be of man's doing, but will far outrun all human expectations. (Mark 4:1-9, 26-29, 30-32; Matt. 13:33; Luke 13:20-21).

THE CRISIS NOW: GOD DEMANDS RADICAL OBEDIENCE

That such grace really undergirds the absolute ethic of Jesus now becomes clear in two ways. First, discipleship rests solely on the personal call of Jesus. It is a personal response to his personal invitation, " Follow me " (Mark 1:17). Second, the demands Jesus makes on those who respond rest solely on his own obedience. He asks those whom he calls simply to identify themselves with him, to accept what he has done, with all the privilege and the hazard that such obedience on their part may bring. Since the call is his and the first act of obedience is his, discipleship is not a goal to be attained, but a gift to be received. What seems to be an impossible demand on his part is not a hurdle to be cleared so that one may enter God's presence. It is, rather, an opportunity for loving response, to test those whom he has called and to instruct them in the nature of their calling.

Jesus' various encounters with Peter, for example, epitomize discipleship as the personal relationship it really is. He rebukes Peter for wishing to avoid suffering (Mark 8:31-35). He instructs him in the nature of forgiveness (Matt. 18:21-22). He prays for him in his time of testing (Luke 22:31-34) and sends him a word of encouragement after his miserable failure (Mark 16:7). By so doing he simply unveils to Peter the way of suffering, forgiveness, and temptation he himself has traveled. It is this pattern of discipleship that separates Jesus from the men of Qumran. The strict regulations of the Essene community set up a closed society and exacted a rigid discipline from its members, whereas the radical demand of Jesus is shaped by his own prior obedience and depends for its execution solely upon the personal response his disciples are willing to give to him as their Lord. This is abundantly evident even when one uses as the basis for such a comparison the highly stereotyped regulations of Matt. 18:1-20. (Contrast Matt. 18:19-20, for example, with 1QS 5:24–6:1; 6:24–7:25; 8:20–9:2.)

If such is the nature of Christian discipleship, surely the place to begin in trying to understand it is with the obedience of Jesus himself. His ministry opens with a time of testing (Matt. 4:1-11) and closes with a prayer of renunciation. " And he said, ' Abba, Father, all things are possible to thee; remove this cup from me; yet not what I will, but what thou wilt.' " (Mark 14:36.) It was to do his father's will that he had come to Jerusalem for the last time. " At that very hour some Pharisees came, and said to him, ' Get away from here, for Herod wants to kill you.' And he said to them, ' Go and tell that fox, " Behold, I cast out demons and perform cures today and tomorrow, and the third day I finish my course. Nevertheless I must go on my way today and tomorrow and the day following; for it cannot be that a prophet should perish away from Jerusalem." ' " (Luke 13:31-33.) " A prophet," he once said, " is not without honor, except in his own country, and among his own kin, and in his own house." (Mark 6:1-6.)

Such obedience led him to heroic action on two fronts. On the one hand, as the chosen emissary of God, he had to reinterpret the ancient law of his people in an independent and radical way, to mediate the divine presence now let loose afresh in his own ministry. Long since, the elect of Qumran had given themselves to a similar task. " And in the place where the ten are, let there not lack a man who studies the Law night and day, continually, concerning the duties of each towards the other. And let the Many watch in common for a third of all the nights of the year, to read the Book and study the law and bless in common " (1QS 6:6-8). Like these devout men, Jesus had to search the Scriptures to discover God's hand in his own ministry, even though this meant rousing the active opposition of Israel's leaders who had their own Scriptural tradition. Thus he broke the Sabbath (Mark 2:23 to 3:6). He put inward purity not alongside of, but in place of, ritual purity (ch. 7:14-23). He forbade divorce completely (ch. 10:1-12). He moved from the bare surface of God's command to the quick of its inward purpose (Matt. 5:21-48). He laid open without flinching the perversion of Israel's religious heritage on the part of her best people (Luke 11:37 to 12:1; Matt. 6:1-18).

On the other hand, he called his disciples into an intimate relationship with himself so that they might perfect the same discipline and endure the same hostility as he. This is what Mark reveals to us in his dramatic description of Jesus' journey toward Jerusalem (Mark 10:35-45). As Jesus travels toward the cross, James and John of his inner circle step forward to solicit special privilege. As part of Jesus' rebuke we read, " You know that those who are supposed to rule over the Gentiles lord it over them, and their great men exercise authority over them. But it shall not be so among you; but whoever would be great among you must be your servant, and whoever would be first among you must be slave of all." In accepting these demands the disciples simply follow their Lord. " For the Son of man also came not to be served but to serve, and to give his life as a ransom for many." (Mark 10:42-45.) How appropriate in this light is Matthew's comment on the apostolic mission. " A disciple is not above his teacher, nor a servant above his master; it is enough for the disciple to be like his teacher, and the servant like his master. If they have called the master of the house Be-elzebub, how much more will they malign those of his household." (Matt. 10:24-25.)

If we can judge from the imperious call that Jesus issues and the immediate response that he gets, this binding relationship existed from the very outset between him and his innermost circle of disciples (Mark 1:6-10; 2:13-17; Luke 5:1-11). It is in the bond of this relationship that they are sent out to continue what Jesus himself had begun. Mark describes this quite clearly (Mark 3:13-15): "And he went up into the hills, and called to him those whom he desired; and they came to him. And he appointed twelve, to be with him, and to be sent out to preach and have authority to cast out demons." They travel under emergency conditions appropriate to the urgency of their message and they are told to expect rejection (Mark 6:6-13). "Go your way," says Jesus, "behold, I send you out as lambs in the midst of wolves." (Luke 10:3.)

We are not surprised to find that such obedience cuts across the normal loyalties of the home, separates men from their wealth, requires enormous faith, and demands forgiveness and love on a gargantuan scale (Mark 11:20-26; Luke 6:27-36; 9:51-56; 10:29-37; 12:13-34; Matt. 6:19-34; 7:7-11; 18:21-35). One example is sufficient to illustrate. Consider Jesus' attitude toward the family. "Do you think," he says, "that I have come to give peace on earth? No, I tell you, but rather division; for henceforth in one house there will be five divided, three against two and two against three. . . . If any one comes to me and does not hate his own father and mother and wife and children and brothers and sisters, yes, and even his own life, he cannot be my disciple." (Luke 12:51-52; 14:26.) But this advice to his disciples simply reflects the situation in which Jesus himself stood. When told on one occasion that his mother and brothers wanted to see him, he responded, "Who are my mother and my brothers? And looking around on those who sat about him, he said, 'Here are my mother and my brothers! Whoever does the will of God is my brother, and sister, and mother.'" (Mark 3:33-35.)

At first glance such austerity seems to fit in well with the strenuous demands that appear in the Beatitudes of Matthew. In the formalized context of Matthew's first discourse, such severe demands seem to frown upon those seeking entrance to the Kingdom as though put there specifically to forbid their going any farther. The price of admission is set so high that only the most noble of men have even the slightest hope of paying it. To view the Beatitudes in this way, however, as throwing up such obstacles, is to misunderstand both Matthew and the pattern of discipleship we have been observing elsewhere. The achievements pictured here are to be understood, rather, as marks of life, the very life that Jesus bestows as a gift upon those who follow him.

Matthew himself quite clearly has this understanding of his own work when he sums up the essence of discipleship in ch. 5:13-16. In each case his imperative is preceded by an indicative. The disciples are declared to be the salt of the earth before they are warned not to lose their savor. Similarly, they are recognized as the light of the world before being asked to hold forth this light in obedience before the world. Still further, the Beatitudes by their very nature reveal the kind of discipleship we have been exploring. The blessings that Jesus bestows upon his own are the fruits of the very life into which he has led them. What is described is not simply what they ought to attain but what he has already attained and now wishes to share with them. It is no accident that all the Beatitudes taken together describe, first of all, the life that Jesus himself lived. Above all others, he himself is the most lowly, most pure, most righteous, and most merciful. Nor is it any accident that the response Jesus expects matches the blessing he has bestowed. He desires only that those he blesses should follow where he leads. The meek, the pure, the peacemakers, the righteous, and above all, the humble and the merciful are the only ones who can really follow Jesus and treasure his blessing. They alone can be salt and light so far as they mediate what he has imparted to them. The fact that the response he expects from them is here tabulated in a formalized way only serves to describe in a more explicit fashion the place where true disciples ought to be standing, once they dare to plumb the depths of the new relationship to which by God's grace they have been admitted.

Most of all, it is just at this point that the Beatitude on persecution finds its rightful place. Here, beyond the shadow of a doubt, the disciples of Jesus are addressed. And here we find what is most characteristic in his appeal to them. Just as they are called to accept his position in this world, so also does he impart to them his joy. His understanding of his own mission and theirs shines through these words with astonishing clarity. Both he and they, having received the good gifts of God, must now open themselves like the prophets of old to the scorn of God's enemies. But God is with them and all will be well. They can be certain that their enemies will not prevail.

The flavor of this final Beatitude could certainly be duplicated in other forms at Qumran since the faith of the Covenanters was also a faith for martyrs. 1QH 2:20-25 is worth quoting as one expression, at least, of sectarian faith under persecution.

> I give Thee thanks, O Adonai,
> for Thou hast placed my soul in the sack of
>   life
> and protected me from all the snares of the
>   Pit!
> Violent men have sought my soul
> because I leaned on Thy Covenant.
> But they are an assembly of vanity
> and a congregation of Belial.
> They knew not that my being proceeds from
>   Thee

and that Thou wilt save my soul by Thy
favours;
for my steps proceed from Thee.
And it is on Thy behalf that they have
threatened my life,
that Thou mightest be glorified by the judgment of the wicked
and manifest Thy power in me before the sons
of men;
for it is by Thy grace that I stand upright.

Once again, the difference between such a noble poem as
this and the Beatitude on persecution lies in Jesus. His life
itself wove a distinctive pattern from the abundant materials to which he and the elect of Qumran had access. Only
if we understand the personal nature of the discipleship he
offered can we understand why the church did not withdraw to the wilderness as did the Essenes and why in the
long run her discipline under persecution proved far more
durable.

THE CRISIS NOW AND THE CRISIS TO COME

If Jesus knew that God had come to visit his people, he
was also confident that God would complete what he had
begun. If he knew that God was pouring out his grace in
revolutionary ways, he believed with all his heart that that
grace would triumph. So he spoke not only of discerning
God's gracious activity in the present (Luke 12:54-56) but
also of preparing for the full exercise of God's rule in the
future. He counseled his disciples to pray, " Thy kingdom
come " (ch. 11:2), and sent them out to proclaim that
that Kingdom was near at hand (Mark 1:15; 6:12; Matt.
10:7; Luke 10:11). He apparently believed that this Kingdom would arrive soon (Mark 13:28-29), so soon that
some of his contemporaries would live to see it (Mark
9:1; Matt. 10:23). Like a tiny mustard seed, God's power

would burst forth until his work was accomplished (Luke 13:18-19). In spite of many obstacles, there would be a tremendous harvest (Mark 4:8).

At the same time, Jesus made no predictions to pinpoint the exact moment when this result would ensue. The timing was entirely in God's hands (Mark 13:30-32). The coming of God's rule would not be heralded by obvious signs of a miraculous sort but would appear quite suddenly (Luke 17:20-24). Its coming would be as sudden as a flash of lightning, taking everyone by surprise (vs. 26-29).

In keeping with this uncertainty, Jesus constantly urged men to be zealous in preparation. All that he says about entering the Kingdom is to be understood in this light. Every word we have on this subject is spoken with the utmost urgency. " Strive to enter by the narrow door; for many, I tell you, will seek to enter and will not be able " (Luke 13:24; Matt. 6:33; 7:13-14, 21). It is better to enter maimed than not to enter at all (Mark 9:43-47). The Pharisees are condemned for hindering many; and riches are an almost insuperable barrier (Matt. 23:13; Mark 10:23). The prime requirement is to humble oneself like a little child (Mark 10:13-16). Coupled with these stern words are a whole series of stories counseling men to be on the alert. Since they know not the hour of their master's arrival nor the hour when the thief will break in, they must always be ready (Luke 12:35-46; 13:22-30; Mark 13:33-37).

As a review of the relevant literature from the bibliography will show, these emphases have been sorely misunderstood. Albert Schweitzer proposed in an epoch-making survey that Jesus had laid such absolute and heavy demands upon men simply because the time was so short. His ethic was intended only for the " interim " between Jesus' proclamation of the Kingdom and its arrival. Instead of allowing for the uncertainties that Jesus himself felt, Schweitzer imposed upon him a consuming interest in apocalyptic detail and an ironclad, somewhat mechanical reading of history. But a strong protest was soon raised by such scholars as C. H. Dodd, Amos Wilder, and W. G. Kümmel, so that we now can view Jesus' expectation for the future in a more balanced way. As Wilder demonstrated, Jesus brought men, not before a final catastrophe, but before God himself. As Dodd showed, this God was already active prior to the end. Both these insights we have sought to take seriously by interpreting the severity of Jesus' ethic in the light of his deep awareness of God's presence. As we put it earlier in this chapter, the gift God bestows in establishing his rule makes his demand for response just that much more urgent. Jesus' " ethics " are therefore Kingdom ethics or discipleship ethics, their absoluteness being occasioned by the radically new situation before God in which Jesus and his disciples find themselves. The corollary of receiving God's unheard-of gift is to feel its unsparing demand upon one's life. This is what pressed upon Jesus and, through him, upon his disciples. Now we want to reaffirm the conclusions of W. G. Kümmel by showing that in Jesus' ministry present and future stand in organic relation under God as the fulfillment of his ancient promise. All that Jesus proposes about the crisis to come grows out of the crisis in whose midst he now stands. All that we propose from this point on will reaffirm such a vital and organic connection. What God promises for the Last Day is already in process of being fulfilled now. Just so, what God does now in Jesus will have its inevitable result in what he will do on the Last Day.

As we have had occasion to observe, it is just this tension between the present and the future that differentiates and yet unites the thought of Jesus and that of Qumran. On the one hand, both do feel this tension quite strongly, but on the other hand, this tension is resolved in quite different ways.

For example, the Qumran sectarians regarded their

prayers and studies as a substitute for the sacrifices of the Jerusalem Temple which according to their standards had been hopelessly corrupted. From this point of view we may understand the following self-description taken from 1QS 8:5-10:

> The Council of the Community shall be established in truth as an everlasting planting.
> It is the House of holiness for Israel
> and the Company of infinite holiness for Aaron;
> they are the witnesses of truth unto Judgment
> and the chosen of Loving-kindness
> appointed to offer expiation for the earth
> and to bring down punishment upon the wicked.
> It is the tried wall, the precious corner-stone;
> its foundations shall not tremble
> nor flee from their place.
> It is the Dwelling of infinite holiness for Aaron
> in (eternal) Knowledge unto the Covenant of justice
> and to make offerings of sweet savour;
> (it is) the House of perfection and truth in Israel
> to establish the Covenant according to the everlasting precepts.
> And they shall be accepted as expiation for the earth
> and to decree the judgment of wickedness
> with no perversity remaining.

Quite clearly the perspective of such a passage embraces both the present and the future. If the glory of the Temple had been transferred to the Essene community, and the members of this community were to act as judges of the wicked in the final judgment, and their performance of ritual and ethical obligations could serve as "an expiation for the earth," all that they were doing prior to the Last Day was preparing them for the functions they would exercise then. If what they were building to substitute for the Temple could be described as holy, infinite, everlasting, true, and perfect, a building whose foundations could not be shaken, then surely the fruit of their work would continue from this age into the next. Likewise we learn that the battle between wickedness and righteousness which will occupy the forty years of Messianic travail (1QM 1:9-14) is a battle that has already begun before that time. By the decree of God, men walk continually by either the spirit of Truth or the spirit of Perversity; and they must war with each other "until the final end" when "at the time of the Visitation" God will destroy Perversity "for ever" (1QS 4:15-20). Once again the view taken by the men of Qumran concerning their existence in this world serves as a fitting preparation for the outcome they envision for the Last Day. In this vein we do not wonder that the sufferings of the Qumran Psalmist merge imperceptibly into the terrors of the last days. In one sense such sufferings might mean that the last days were very near or indeed had already begun. (Compare 1QH 3:19-28a with the subsequent verses, 28b-36.)

It is just such expectations that we must keep in mind as we now investigate more thoroughly what Jesus had to say about the future. For the moment it is sufficient to recall what we have already learned. Jesus is already aware that God's victory over Satan has begun, whereas the elect of Qumran can do nothing but wait for it. Moreover, we do not find in Jesus the apocalyptic program of Qumran's forty year Holy War, nor the thirst for revenge that motivates it. His eschatology is not so sharply apocalyptic as theirs. He is not interested in imparting bizarre information about the sudden action that God will take to interrupt forever the course of history. He is simply content to

prepare men for what God has in store, knowing that in
his own time God will bring to fruition the seeds he himself has planted.

THE JUDGMENT TO COME

If the men of Qumran felt that they were destined to
judge the nations in the last times, we may now ask in
more detail what picture Jesus had of the judgment to
come.

Since John the Baptist had such definite convictions on
this subject we may begin with him. Although Jesus had
quite a different message than John, he did accept John's
baptism, and it was the purpose of that baptism to prepare
Israel for total and consuming judgment at God's hands
(Matt. 3:7-12). In a unique sacramental way a remnant of
true Israelites must purge themselves in advance by water
in order to withstand the final purging by fire through
which Israel must inevitably pass (v. 12). Something of
this experience reappears in Jesus' reformulation of his
own destiny.

At some point in his ministry Jesus understood that the
Kingdom would come in fullness only through some great
personal sacrifice on his part. According to Mark 1:14 he
began his work in the shadow of John's death, as though
this were also to be his lot. According to Luke's version of
Jesus' rejection at Nazareth (Luke 4:16-30; Mark 6:1-6),
this moment was to be typical of his whole ministry. In one
moment of great anguish we hear Jesus cry out: " I came
to cast fire upon the earth; and would that it were already
kindled! I have a baptism to be baptized with; and how I
am constrained until it is accomplished! " (Luke 12:49-
50). However formalized by the Evangelist, the Marcan
predictions of Jesus' passion bear eloquent testimony to Jesus' premonition of death (Mark 8:31-33; 9:9-13, 30-32;
10:32-34, 45). At the very least they show how conscious

he was of the precarious position in which he stood. He would suffer and be betrayed (Luke 17:25; Mark 9:12; 14:21). This is not to suggest that Jesus regarded such suffering as a judgment upon himself. It does suggest, however, that he was keenly aware how rebellious his people had been, how deserving they were of the wrath John had announced, and how deeply involved he must become in their fate.

It is in keeping with this awareness that we have from Jesus quite explicit warnings concerning judgment to come. He does not spell out the details, but he is quite certain about the fact itself. What is more important, he always sees this judgment to come in relation to the rejection he himself is experiencing. As we have pointed out repeatedly in analyzing his thought, the crisis to come grows out of and reflects the crisis in the midst of which he stands. Judgment is certain only because God's grace has been so surely offered and so firmly rejected. For Jesus, judgment to come was no stereotyped dogma but the solemn pang of the bitter cup his own countrymen were forcing him to drink.

This is true, for example, of the preaching mission he and his disciples undertake. Even in the moment of their proclaiming the Kingdom, the issue is decisively drawn. When they are received, the peace of God can be offered, and when they are repulsed, judgment is already certain (Matt. 10:11-16, 21-23; 11:20-24; Luke 10:5-16). When men foolishly look for miraculous signs, they miss completely the challenge Jesus himself has brought. He himself is the only sign they are to receive — the sign of Jonah (Luke 11:29-30). But this they do not accept and therefore open themselves to greater condemnation than the men of Nineveh. "The men of Nineveh will arise at the judgment with this generation and condemn it; for they repented at the preaching of Jonah, and behold, something greater than Jonah is here." (Matt. 12:38-42; 16:1-4;

Mark 8:11-13; Luke 11:29-32.) They know what to do when caught by an accuser, but not when confronted by God (Luke 12:54-59). Unlike the unjust steward whom Jesus commended, they have no wisdom in adjusting themselves to the visitation of God (ch. 16:1-8).

Confronted by such rebellion, Jesus' premonition of judgment to come embraces the whole nation. In three familiar parables he calls up all the ancient imagery of his people to make his warning to them as explicit as possible. The fig tree that bears no fruit must be cut down (Luke 13:1-9). The tenants who withhold the fruits of their master's vineyard must be replaced (Mark 12:1-12). The guests who refuse to come when invited shall never taste the banquet prepared for them (Luke 14:15-24). This generation shall receive the accumulated woes of all of Israel's past (Matt. 23:32-36). Jerusalem itself will perish (Luke 13:34-35; 17:31; 19:39-44; 21:20-24), and the Temple of God will be torn down (Mark 13:1-2).

Here we are reminded of the Woes of Luke. Together with his Beatitudes they assign to God the same free-ranging sovereignty that we see here in Jesus' premonition of judgment. The Lord God is Lord of Israel and he will not be denied! He will root up and overturn, he will lift up and tear down, and none shall stay his hand. Once more we are reminded of Jesus' robust concern for the whole of his people and we are transported by his words into the presence of a prophet like Amos:

Hear this word that the Lord has spoken against you, O people of Israel, against the whole family which I brought up out of the land of Egypt:

> " You only have I known
>   of all the families of the earth;
> therefore I will punish you
>   for all your iniquities."
>   (Amos 3:1-2)

In some sense Jesus and Qumran stand here on the same footing. Each predicts severe judgment at God's hands for Israel and each makes his own experience with God the criterion for it. Through their study of the Old Testament both speak with prophetic voice as God's appointed messengers to his people. At the same time, the scheme of judgment proposed by the elect of Qumran is shot through with a rigid, narrow determinism that is quite foreign to Jesus. Ponder for a moment this Essene interpretation of Habakkuk which exalts their alleged purity in order to establish them as judges both of their own countrymen and of the Gentiles (1QpHab. 5:3-8) : " The explanation of this word is that God will not destroy His people by the hand of the nations; but God will judge all the nations by the hand of His elect. And it is by the chastisement which the elect will dispense that all the wicked of His people will atone, because they (the elect) have kept His commandments in their distress. For it is as He said, *With eyes too pure to see evil.* The explanation of this is that they let not themselves be led astray into lewdness by their eyes during the time of wickedness."

MERCY FOR THE GENTILES

Once again the profound difference between Jesus and Qumran may be measured by his attitude toward the Gentiles, and once again his activities as teacher and healer set the pattern for his thinking about the future. Thus, when the occasion presents itself, we find him ministering to the Roman centurion (Luke 7:1-10) and the Syro-Phoenician woman (Mark 7:24-30). It is equally noteworthy that Jesus felt no hatred for Israel's enemies. He did not respond with vengeance when told of the Jews massacred in Galilee by Pilate (Luke 13:1-3), nor when refused entrance to a Samaritan village (ch. 9:51-56). He went out of his way to praise Samaritan virtue (ch. 10:29-37; 17:11-19). He counseled submission to Roman taxes (Matt. 5:41; Mark 12:13-17) and chose a tax collector as one of his disciples (Mark 2:13-17).

This openhearted spirit is what we find also in Jesus' descriptions of the future. Although most Jews under the heel of Roman domination felt that God would punish the Gentiles at the Last Day, Jesus did not feel this way. He agreed with John the Baptist that Jewish blood would not save his countrymen from God's wrath (Luke 3:7-9; 13:6-9; 16:26). " All the nations " will be treated at God's seat of judgment solely with regard to their deeds (Matt. 25:31-46). What is more astonishing, Jesus proposed that the Jews by virtue of rejecting him would be put to shame in the judgment by the Gentiles — by Tyre and Sidon (Luke 10:13-14), by Sodom (Matt. 11:23-24), by Nineveh, and by the Queen of Sheba (Luke 11:31-32). Beyond even this, Jesus suggested that the Gentiles might even receive mercy at the expense of the Jews. So we learn from Jesus' address at Nazareth that Elijah passed over the widows of Israel in favor of a Gentile widow from Sidon, and Elisha denied the lepers in Israel by ministering only to Naaman the Syrian (Luke 4:25-27). With one bold sweeping gesture Jesus puts such a lesson from history to work when he paints his picture of the final Messianic feast. Then, he predicted, " many " would come " from east and west and sit at table with Abraham, Isaac, and Jacob in the kingdom of heaven, while the sons of the kingdom " would be cast aside " into the outer darkness " (Matt. 8:11-12).

We must ponder with great care such an expectation so powerfully fashioned. Jesus' use of such an image leads us into the broad reaches of the Old Testament where again and again it is said that God will commune in festive banquet with his own (Ps. 23:5-6) and where it is also said that the Gentiles will come to Mt. Zion in the last days to enjoy such fellowship (Isa. 25:6-9; 49:1-13). It is important to keep these images in mind, particularly when we seek to

explain the bewildering events by which Jesus' life came to
its close. Then, if ever, we should have some reflection of
Jesus' hope for the future, some reading of his mind to indicate how he thought it would all turn out. The cleansing
of the Temple may well furnish some such indication.
Mark 11:17, following Isa. 56:7 and Jer. 7:11, explicitly
says that Jesus' purpose was to make the Court of the Gentiles once more accessible to them. But then, even without
this specific reference, any cleansing of the old Temple in
this symbolic way would suggest that the time had come
for the establishment of a new Temple where all men
might worship the God of Israel on Mt. Zion. Isaiah 56:1-8
and ch. 19:19-25 herald this lofty hope in vivid and positive terms. Bertil Gärtner in his book *The Temple and
the Community in Qumran and the New Testament* shows
quite clearly that both Jesus and the men of Qumran expected the Temple not to be completely destroyed but
only replaced. Whereas the Essene Covenanters felt that
the purified worship of their own community would re-
place the corruption of the Temple hierarchy, Jesus, on
the contrary, pointed to himself and his disciples as the
new place where God would meet his people (Matt. 12:6;
Mark 14:57-58).

If we take seriously such revolutionary thoughts, it may
help us to explain further the prophetic symbolism of Jesus' entry into Jerusalem. What could he hope to accomplish by this otherwise quixotic gesture if not to broadcast
in unmistakable terms that the time had come for a king
who would " command peace to the nations " (Zech. 9:9-
10) ? Behind the perplexing nexus of events surrounding
the end of Jesus' life, however difficult they are to interpret in detail, we may sense his expectation that God
would soon move to turn the existing order upside down.
We must remember not simply that Jesus cleansed the
Temple but that he somehow raised the expectation that
if the present Temple were destroyed, he would build it

anew (Mark 14:57-58). We must remember not simply his prediction that many would come to sit at table with Abraham, Isaac, and Jacob in the Kingdom but his equally strong expectation that both he and his disciples would sit down with them (v. 25).

THE GREAT REVERSAL

There are a number of sayings attributed to Jesus in the tradition that not only relate the present to the future in a general way but declare that the events of the future will reverse completely the course of life experienced in the present. We have called this the great reversal in order to bring out in bold relief one of the most prominent of Jesus' convictions. In their own way the Qumran Covenanters expected something of the same thing. Though persecuted and " poor " they expected to be honored in the last times both as warriors who would overcome wickedness and as judges who would condemn it. We may now inquire in what way Jesus formulated his expectations differently.

We learn, for example, that what men decide about Jesus now will put them in the hands of God at the judgment (Luke 10:16; Mark 9:37). As Matthew puts it, " He who receives you receives me, and he who receives me receives him who sent me " (Matt. 10:40). Those who assent to Jesus' message now will be accepted by God on the Last Day, whereas those who deny him will be rejected at that time (Luke 12:8-9; Matt. 10:32-33). But this means that what is hidden now will only come to light later on (Luke 12:2-3; Mark 4:22; Matt. 10:26-27). Although it is not clear now whether Jesus had been sent by God, this will be put beyond doubt at the judgment. " Whatever you have said in the dark shall be heard in the light." (Luke 12:3a.) Thus it is that those who respond now will be in a more favorable position then, and those who do not respond now will be even worse off then. It is in this light that we should read Mark 4:25 and the series of statements related to it (Luke 12:47-48; 19:26; Matt. 25:29). " And he said to them, 'Take heed what you hear; the measure you give will be the measure you get, and still more will be given you. For to him who has will more be given; and from him who has not, even what he has will be taken away.' " (Mark 4:24-25.)

Such teaching cuts a wide swathe in our records of Jesus' life, particularly where he insists on humility. When, for example, we read Luke 14:7-14 it seems as though Jesus were simply giving prudential advice on how one should act at a wedding. " When you are invited by any one to a marriage feast, do not sit down in a place of honor." (V. 8a.) But it soon becomes obvious that this wedding feast is meant to suggest that final feast to which, as we have seen, God will invite all men. It is particularly for " the poor," " the maimed," " the lame," and " the blind " (v. 13), the very ones for whom God has the greatest concern. More important is the principle that this whole teaching sets forth. It is not simply a question of good manners or psychological receptivity or social prejudice, but the fact that in the last analysis all men stand or fall before God. He will set matters straight as the final judge of the world. " For every one who exalts himself will be humbled, and he who humbles himself will be exalted." (V. 11.) It is on this basis that one enters the Kingdom (Mark 10:13-16) or finds his place in it (Matt. 18:1-5; 23:8-12). It is on this basis that God will deal with those who exclude themselves from it (Luke 16:14-15; 18:9-14). So we read that those who would be first must put themselves last (Mark 9:35) and we also read that God himself will finally establish all things in this way. "And behold, some are last who will be first, and some are first who will be last." (Luke 13:30; cf. Mark 10:31; Matt. 19:30).

In this vein we have the general assurance that God does

hear and will vindicate those who appeal to him at the Last Day (Luke 18:1-8). More specifically, God's great reversal of fortune is particularly illustrated by reference to Jesus and his disciples. Though humbled now, they and he will eat together at the banquet table of God's Kingdom (Luke 22:28-30; Mark 14:25). Though scattered now, his flock shall be gathered and given their rightful inheritance (Luke 12:32; Mark 14:27-28). Though despised now and few in number, they will be allowed to occupy thrones of judgment in the age to come (Luke 22:30; Matt. 19:28; Mark 10:40).

Surely it is in this light we must interpret the eschatological tension resident in the Beatitudes. Those who hunger now shall be filled! In both Gospels, whether confined to disciples or broadened to include the whole of Israel, the Beatitudes declare this great reversal of fortune in no uncertain terms.

THE SON OF MAN

If Jesus did expect God to turn things upside down — to exalt the humble and humble the exalted, to give the Gentiles an even better place in the Kingdom than the Jews — nothing expresses this conviction more powerfully than what he said about the Son of Man.

In the Gospel tradition we find *three separate groupings* of passages relating the term " Son of Man " respectively to his appearance in glory, to his death and resurrection, and to his humble life on earth.

In group I, we find such verses as Mark 13:26-27, " And then they will see the Son of man coming in clouds with great power and glory. And then he will send out the angels, and gather his elect from the four winds, from the ends of the earth to the ends of heaven." Characteristic of group II is Mark 8:31, where Jesus speaks to his disciples after the confession of Peter to set the pattern for his subsequent ministry. " And he began to teach them that the Son of man must suffer many things, and be rejected by the elders and the chief priests and the scribes, and be killed, and after three days rise again." In group III, we find such statements as this discipleship word from Luke 9:58, " And Jesus said to him, ' Foxes have holes, and birds of the air have nests; but the Son of man has nowhere to lay his head.' "

No less important than these three groupings within the Synoptic material are the *three major meanings* we may assign to the term itself from the various contexts in which it occurs in relevant Jewish literature. Sometimes the term, particularly in its Aramaic form, may mean simply " man " in a generic sense. Thus we read in Ps. 8:4, " What is man that thou art mindful of him, and the son of man that thou dost care for him? " In another sense " son of man " simply singles out a specific individual such as the prophet Ezekiel. The term is used some eighty-seven times in the book bearing his name to describe him in all his activities as God's messenger to Israel. " And he said to me, ' Son of man, stand upon your feet, and I will speak with you.' And when he spoke to me, the Spirit entered into me and set me upon my feet; and I heard him speaking to me. And he said to me, ' Son of man, I send you to the people of Israel, to a nation of rebels, who have rebelled against me; they and their fathers have transgressed against me to this very day.' " (Ezek. 2:1-3.)

If these first two meanings may be labeled " generic " and " individual," the phrase " son of man " also occurs in a " collective " sense. As such it is a poetic way of designating the whole nation of Israel. Thus we read of Israel in Ps. 80:17:

> But let thy hand be upon the man
>   of thy right hand,
> the son of man whom thou hast
>   made strong for thyself!

This collective sense is transposed to an apocalyptic key in Dan. 7:13-14, where over against the beasts that symbolize pagan kingdoms Israel is addressed as the Son of Man, and her triumph in the midst of persecution is predicted.

> I saw in the night visions,
> > and behold, with the clouds of heaven
> > > there came one like a son of man,
> > and he came to the Ancient of Days
> > > and was presented before him.
> > And to him was given dominion
> > > and glory and kingdom
> > that all peoples, nations, and languages
> > > should serve him;
> > his dominion is an everlasting dominion,
> > > which shall not pass away,
> > and his kingdom one
> > > that shall not be destroyed.

It seems that this phrase also appears prominently in I Enoch (consult in particular chs. 46; 48; 62; 63; 69 to 71), but it is not clear there whether the figure so addressed is individual or collective, or in what sense the term is individualized by its possible reference to Enoch himself at I Enoch 71:14.

In view of such varied data, both within and outside the Synoptics, it is small wonder that scholars disagree about its interpretation. Since " Son of Man " does not often occur in the same context as the phrase " Kingdom of God," some scholars cut the two asunder and assign only the latter to Jesus. For most scholars, however, this seems too drastic, since in all of its seventy or more occurrences in the Gospels it rests only on the lips of Jesus. At the same time it could hardly have originated in the later church since it occurs outside the Gospels only in Acts 7:56 and Rev. 1:13 and 14:14.

Assuming that Jesus did use the term, *three basic interpretations* are currently proposed for it, each taking its cue from one of the three groupings of Synoptic data described at the outset.

A. Such scholars as John Knox and Rudolf Bultmann lay major stress on the sayings in group I. They point out that this group is the most numerous and that it occurs in all the Synoptic sources — Mark, Q, M, and L — whereas group II is confined to Mark. They also make much of the fact that group I can be easily separated from group II, there being only one passage where the Parousia and the suffering of the Son of Man are joined (Luke 17:25). All in all, these scholars conclude, Jesus spoke only about the coming of the Son of Man in glory. He did so in the third person, not wishing to identify himself with this exalted figure. However, when the church recorded the sayings it made the identification that Jesus refused to make either by freely editorializing (as in Matt. 13:37) or by replacing an original " I " with " Son of Man " (as in ch. 16:13).

B. Such scholars as T. W. Manson, Vincent Taylor, and Reginald Fuller use passages from all three groupings but place major emphasis on those from group II. According to their interpretation, Jesus thinks of himself as Son of Man even during his lifetime. He also looks forward to his fulfillment of the Son of Man's destiny in glory. This view of his ministry rises from Jesus' understanding of two images: the suffering servant in Isaiah and the Son of Man in Daniel. By combining such motifs Jesus intends to emphasize the particular kind of Messianic role he is to play in contrast to contemporary expectations. He alone will deserve Messianic dignity by sacrificing himself for his people (Mark 10:45). For Fuller, the Kingdom does not come until after the cross. Before dying on the cross Jesus suffers only as the Son of Man designate.

C. A third interpretation is proposed by Eduard Schweizer, of Zurich, mainly on the basis of passages from group III. Schweizer moves from what he regards as a significant contrast in Jewish thought between humiliation and exaltation. According to this pattern, he can claim that Jesus is Son of Man both in suffering and in glory but he can also give to this claim a somewhat different meaning than any we have yet encountered. The following examples will make this clear:

Luke 7:34 describes the Son of Man as " a glutton and a drunkard, a friend of tax collectors and sinners." Such an uncomplimentary judgment, so unfavorable to Jesus and so favorable to the Baptist, undoubtedly reveals Jesus' own use of this term and not that of the early church. If one joins to this perspective the phrase quoted earlier from ch. 9:58 that " the Son of man has nowhere to lay his head," one catches the spirit of the prophet Ezekiel. Such a one can be, like Jonah, a sign to his own generation. " For as Jonah became a sign to the men of Nineveh, so will the Son of man be to this generation." (Ch. 11:30.) In the same way a parallel can be drawn between the earthly ministry of Jesus and that of righteous Noah before the flood. " As it was in the days of Noah, so will it be in the days of the Son of man." (Ch. 17:26.) By laying special weight on such passages as these, Schweizer opens up a new line of approach. Although he agrees with Taylor and Manson that Jesus described himself in all his lowliness as " Son of Man," he bypasses almost entirely the Marcan passion sayings (chs. 8:31; 9:12; 9:31; 10:45) on which their interpretation lays such stress. Schweizer does agree, however, that the predicted rejection of Mark 8:31 does ring true, particularly since it is joined to the vivid protest and rebuke at v. 33. Such a strong rebuke of so prominent a person as Peter could hardly have been invented! Along with this certainly authentic passage are to be read other passages predicting suffering and death for the Son of Man (Luke 17:25; Mark 9:12) and stating that he is to be " betrayed " (Mark 14:21, 41). In all these ways, according to Schweizer, the life of Jesus reincarnates the pattern of righteous suffering so prominent in Jewish thought. Indeed it is just this that justifies our singling out for special attention such passages as Luke 7:34; 9:58; 11:30; and 17:26.

In full accord with the Jewish pattern thus preserved in such passages, our sources also tell us that this lowly Son of Man is destined not only for betrayal but also for triumph. He will appear as witness against his tormentors on the Day of Judgment. This is the sense to be gathered first of all from Luke 12:8, "And I tell you, every one who acknowledges me before men, the Son of man also will acknowledge before the angels of God." Likewise, Mark 14:62 from the trial of Jesus declares the exaltation of this august witness on the Last Day in the presence of God. So far as he thus admits some connection between "Son of Man" and the exaltation of Jesus, Schweizer agrees with all the other interpreters we have discussed. However, such a glorification of Jesus as Schweizer conceives is not his "return," his "coming," or his "Parousia," as the other interpreters have maintained. It is, rather, his vindication. By conceiving the glorification of Jesus only in these terms Schweizer brings out the peculiar flavor of his contention. For Schweizer, Jesus thought of himself as the lowly righteous man in Israel who would be exalted on the Day of Judgment to bear witness against his unrighteous accusers. Mark 14:62 thus uses Dan. 7:13-14 in its primary sense. Into the teeth of his accusers who now condemn him as a criminal Jesus throws this challenge. Just as the "Son of Man" in Daniel was accepted by God at the expense of his pagan persecutors, so also would the work of Jesus gain acceptance at God's hands in spite of his detractors. "'Are you the Christ, the Son of the Blessed?' And Jesus said, 'I am; and you will see the Son of man sitting at the right hand of Power, and coming with the clouds of heaven.'" (Mark 14:62.)

For the time being, this third interpretation by Schweizer seems more acceptable than the others. Though it does not answer all our questions, it rests on solid foundations. On the one hand, it gets behind the witness of the early church to a time when neither the resurrection of Jesus nor his Parousia were expected in the form later treasured by such a thinker as Paul. Could it be that Jesus accepted the lot of suffering as traditionally understood for the righteous in Israel and spoke not of his resurrection or Parousia but of his vindication at the Last Judgment? On the other hand, if Jesus used the term " Son of Man," as Schweizer proposes, we then have from his lips one more reason for that great reversal of fortune which he heralded so eloquently, so often, in so many other ways. Moreover, Schweizer's major contention finds impressive support in both pre-Christian Judaism and in certain Christian traditions outside the Synoptics. The theme Schweizer finds so central is that of humiliation and exaltation. The righteous who suffer in this life will be raised up at the final judgment to bear witness against their tormentors. Now, as we have seen for ourselves, this is one of those areas of experience where Jesus and the elect of Qumran stand side by side. On the basis of the Old Testament both appeal to God as the one who will vindicate his own, who will turn their present sorrow into joy. This is also the motif behind Dan. 7:13-14, and it is exemplified in the case of Enoch by I Enoch, ch. 71; Jubilees 10:17 and 4:23. It appears also in The Wisdom of Solomon 2:11-20; 5:1-5. Without the title " Son of Man," the theme of humiliation and exaltation is picked up by the early hymn lying behind Phil. 2:5-11. The same verb root for exaltation occurs in both the Gospel of John (chs. 3:14; 8:28; 12:32, 34) and Acts (chs. 2:33; 5:31) . Most striking of all is the vision of Acts 7:56 in which Stephen beholds the Son of Man exalted at God's right hand.

THE BEATITUDES IN THE TEACHING OF JESUS

We are now prepared to sum up. Jesus lived in the full flush of God's power as a perfectly obedient Son. As such he could mediate the powers of God's Kingdom long before it had reached its fruition. He could offer now in his blessing what Qumran might only hope for in the Messianic time.

But Jesus was rejected by his own generation. For those who turned against him he predicted judgment but for those who were willing to listen he forsaw complete vindication. God would turn all things upside down, making the first last and the last first, with particular mercy for the outcasts in Israel and the Gentiles. Jesus accepted his humble station with the full assurance that he and the righteous remnant whom he was preparing would be exalted at God's right hand. To express this conviction he chose the term " Son of Man," whether from Ezekiel or Daniel or the Psalms or all three together. It was sufficiently vague to prevent his being taken for a Davidic Messiah with vengeful intent. It was sufficiently clear so that those who would might penetrate his meaning by faith. Above all, it could be used to express the tension between now and then, between humiliation and exaltation, between rejection and vindication, between the one who used it and the many whom he hoped would stand with him on the Last Day. It is this meaning that has become most clear in our day.

We remind ourselves for one last time that here, in his own way, Jesus does express the faith of Qumran that God will vindicate those who trust in him. In this respect they are alike. As God's poor they cry to him for aid or affirm his might before their enemies. But need we also say once again that Jesus proceeds without the exclusiveness, the warlike vengeance, the rigid determinism, or the apocalyptic fancies of the Essene hope? How impossible on his lips would be the following address to God ascribed to the

Qumran High Priest as encouragement for the elect before
their final battle.

> Arise, O Valiant One!
> Lead away Thy captives, O glorious Man!
> Do Thy plundering, O Valorous One!
> Set Thy hand upon the neck of Thine enemies
> and Thy foot upon the heap of the slain!
>   (1QM 12:10-11.)

Since Jesus interprets his exorcism as a victory over Satan,
it must be admitted that to this extent his outlook does
reflect some sort of cosmic dualism. Likewise his conviction that God would effect a great reversal of fortune in
the future does indicate his having set some sort of distinction between an age of sorrow and one of bliss. But he
did not elaborate such a plan for cosmic warfare as we
find in the Scrolls nor does his distinction between the
ages appear as part of a predetermined cosmic scheme. Although he speaks of twelve thrones for his disciples (Matt.
19:28) and a new Temple (Mark 14:57-58) and a gathered flock (Luke 12:32), none of these images is elabo-
rated and none gets its meaning from a stereotyped apocalyptic pattern. All that Jesus asks is that men make up
their minds about him. They must choose what to do with
this lowly Son of Man, being certain only that what they
decide now will be openly confirmed by God on the Last
Day.

It is this tension between present lowliness and future
glory that comes to the fore so wonderfully in the Beatitudes, in both Matthew's version and that of Luke. Upon
the obedient, the pure, and the humble, whose triumph
like his own is not yet evident, he can indeed pronounce a
blessing. He can assure them of open vindication at the
Last Day — that the meek will inherit the earth and the
merciful find mercy and the righteous receive their fill.
Even beyond this, as Luke seems to indicate, he can also

give this assurance to all God's dispossessed in Israel, whether they deserve it or not, solely on the basis of God's sovereign mercy.

We cannot take leave of the Beatitudes without one final comment on Luke 6:21, " Blessed are you that hunger now, for you shall be satisfied." The image of the Messianic banquet expounded here is one of Jesus' favorites. It was through this medium that he spoke of God's intention to invite into his Kingdom the poor, the maimed, the blind, and the lame (Luke 14:13, 21). It was through this medium that he threw open the gates of the Kingdom to the Gentiles (Matt. 8:11). It was through this medium that he expressed his fond hope for reunion with his disciples after his death (Mark 14:25). We are not surprised to find that the banquet image is one of the most powerful in the whole of the Old Testament to express the covenant relation between God and his people. Undoubtedly when Jesus pronounced this second Beatitude, on whatever occasion, he had in mind some such glad invitation as we find at Isa. 55:1, 3. " Ho, every one who thirsts, come to the waters; and he who has no money, come, buy and eat! . . . Hearken diligently to me, and eat what is good, and delight yourselves in fatness."

Once again the contrast with Qumran is striking. We know that every meal at Qumran involved the whole community, was held in a special room, and had a sacred character. No outsider, no novice, and no members under censure were allowed to participate. Each member present was seated acccording to his rank in the society, with the priest as presiding officer. In a similar fashion one's rank determined when he could eat and when he could speak (1QS 6:1-6). According to a similar description in an appendix to their Manual of Discipline (1QSa 2:17-22), it is also probable that such an orderly arrangement was intended to anticipate a similar meal to be held in the Messianic Age, when the Messiah himself would preside, so that

the daily ritual at Qumran also had eschatological overtones (compare Luke 22:16). This is all quite understand-
able in the light of the text we reviewed earlier (4QpPs 37
2:10-11), where the men of Qumran as the Congregation
of the Poor look forward in the last times to being fed as
God's flock on his holy hill.

Although Jesus shares with the elect of Qumran this central image of the banquet, how differently he employs its
richness. With him there is no attempt to exclude the un-
worthy nor any prescribed order for speaking, eating, or
sitting. Rather, he goes out of his way to offend his fellow
countrymen by purposely seeking out as his dinner com-
panions those whom they counted unfit for such communion. When they criticized him, he replied, " Those who
are well have no need of a physician, but those who are
sick; I came not to call the righteous, but sinners " (Mark
2:13-17). Even before the judgment Jesus can take upon
himself the lot of the lowly by sitting down to eat with
publicans and sinners. That he, the Son of Man, should be
found at table with such outcasts is exactly what we should
expect. In hiddenness and humility he proclaims by prophetic symbolism what God shall reveal to all men at the
Last Day when he invites to his great feast those who have
fallen. Every time Jesus is found in such company it is as
though we hear him saying once again, " Blessed are you
poor, for yours is the kingdom of God. Blessed are you
that hunger now, for you shall be satisfied." (Luke 6:20-21.)

BIBLIOGRAPHY

SCHWEIZER'S SURVEY BROUGHT UP TO DATE

Lundström, Gösta, *The Kingdom of God in the Teaching of
Jesus,* tr. by Joan Bulman. John Knox Press, 1963.

McCown, Chester C., *The Search for the Real Jesus.* Charles
Scribner's Sons, 1940.

Perrin, Norman, *The Kingdom of God in the Teaching of
Jesus.* The Westminster Press, 1963.

THE DEBATE OVER ESCHATOLOGY

Beasley-Murray, George R., *Jesus and the Future*. London: Macmillan & Co., Ltd., 1954. Able reaction against modern consensus.

Cullmann, Oscar, *Christ and Time*, rev. ed., tr. by Floyd V. Filson. The Westminster Press, 1964.

Dibelius, Martin, *Jesus*, tr. by Charles B. Hedrick and Frederick C. Grant. The Westminster Press, 1949.

Dodd, C. H., *The Parables of the Kingdom*, rev. ed. Charles Scribner's Sons, 1961.

Jeremias, Joachim, *Jesus' Promise to the Nations*, tr. by S. H. Hooke (Studies in Biblical Theology, No. 24). Alec R. Allenson, Inc., 1958.

Kümmel, Werner G., *Promise and Fulfillment*, tr. by Dorothea M. Barton (Studies in Biblical Theology, No. 23). Alec R. Allenson, Inc., 1957.

Ladd, George E., *Jesus and the Kingdom: The Eschatology of Biblical Realism*. Harper & Row, Publishers, Inc., 1964. Cf. review by N. Perrin, *Interpretation*, XIX (April, 1965), pp. 228–231.

Manson, T. W., *The Servant-Messiah*. Paperback. Cambridge: Cambridge University Press, 1961.

Otto, Rudolf, *The Kingdom of God and the Son of Man*, new and rev. ed., tr. by Floyd V. Filson and Bertram Lee-Woolf. London: Lutterworth Press, 1943.

Percy, E., *Die Botschaft Jesu*. Lund, 1953.

Robinson, John A. T., *Jesus and His Coming*. Abingdon Press, 1957.

Schnackenburg, Rudolf, *God's Rule and Kingdom*, tr. by John Murray. Herder & Herder, Inc., 1963.

Schweitzer, Albert, *The Quest of the Historical Jesus: A Critical Study of Its Progress from Reimarus to Wrede*, tr. from 1st German ed. of 1906 by W. Montgomery. Paperback. The Macmillan Company, 1961.

Taylor, Vincent, *The Life and Ministry of Jesus*. Abingdon Press, 1955.

Wilder, Amos, *Eschatology and Ethics in the Teaching of Jesus*, rev. ed. Harper & Brothers, 1950.

THE SON OF MAN

Black, Matthew, "The Son of Man Problem in Recent Research and Debate," *Bulletin of the John Rylands Library,* XLV (March, 1963), pp. 305–318.

Bowman, John Wick, *The Intention of Jesus.* The Westminster Press, 1943.

Cullmann, Oscar, *The Christology of the New Testament.* The Westminster Press, 1959.

Fuller, Reginald, *The Mission and Achievement of Jesus* (Studies in Biblical Theology, No. 12). Alec R. Allenson, Inc., 1954.

Higgins, A. J. B., *Jesus and the Son of Man.* Fortress Press, 1965.

Knox, John, *The Death of Christ.* Abingdon Press, 1958.

Manson, William, *Jesus the Messiah.* The Westminster Press, 1946.

Schweizer, Eduard, *Lordship and Discipleship* (Studies in Biblical Theology, No. 28). Alec R. Allenson, Inc., 1960.

—— "The Son of Man," *Journal of Biblical Literature,* LXXIX (June, 1960), pp. 119–129.

—— "The Son of Man Again," *New Testament Studies,* IX (April, 1963), pp. 256–261.

Tödt, Heinz Eduard, *The Son of Man in the Synoptic Tradition.* The Westminster Press, 1965.

VII · The Interpreter's Stance:
His Angle of Vision

ESCHATOLOGY AND EXISTENTIALISM IN BULTMANN

OUR INTERPRETATION OF THE BEATITUDES THUS FAR HAS NOT taken formal notice of the most celebrated contribution of perhaps the most influential New Testament scholar of our generation, Rudolf Bultmann. His revolutionary approach and the special meanings he gives to traditional terminology require our listening to him with exceeding care. In a word, Bultmann accepts and sharpens Schweitzer's eschatological understanding of Jesus, but interprets that eschatology in an existentialist way. The future of which Jesus speaks, however garbed in the traditional symbols of Jewish apocalyptic, does not point to some far off, world-shaking event, but to the demand of God that is always breaking in from the immediate future upon our immediate present. Likewise, the present of which Jesus speaks is the decision-making present of his hearers whose openness to the future and real selfhood can only be guaranteed by their responding to Jesus' word now. Bultmann's *Jesus and the Word* deals in three main sections with Jesus' apocalyptic preaching, his ethical teaching, and his existential awareness. Bultmann proceeds from one layer of analysis to the other to show in effect that with each layer we get closer to the real Jesus. We have here a classic example of the process of demythologizing. The eschatological myth is first described in its fullness, and its meaning and function are then gradually unfolded. According to Bultmann, myth does not intend to describe the mighty acts of God as objective realities but simply, in this case, to express how men visualize their relationship to God, to history, to the world, and to each other. By demythologizing we have approached Jesus' teaching not psychologically but ontologically at the deepest level of human existence. It is here that the present and the future take on their existentialist meaning as my present and my future. What seems in traditional eschatology to make a declaration about God ends (when properly demythologized) by describing man at the very core of his being. Existentialist analysis shifts the focus of traditional eschatology from outward events to reality in depth, from the mighty acts of God to man's struggle for authentic selfhood, from theology to anthropology.

THE CHALLENGE OF THE NEW QUEST

In recent years, the pupils of Bultmann, themselves distinguished scholars, have brought his treatment of Jesus under increasing criticism and called for substantial modifications. Since their work also deserves much more attention than we have the space to give, it is to be hoped that the bibliography appended to this chapter will introduce Bultmann, his students, and their basic concerns to the attentive reader. We concentrate here on just one of their most articulate spokesmen, whose book and articles (again as indicated in the bibliography) should give American students a sympathetic appreciation of the " new quest."

James M. Robinson, of the Southern California School of Theology at Claremont, has described this effort in detail in his book *A New Quest of the Historical Jesus.* This quest is new because it repudiates the great nineteenth century attempt to write a full scale life of Jesus. The original quest was impossible and should not be resumed since the Gospels as kerygmatic proclamation simply do not sup-

ply adequate biographical information for it. This quest
was also illegitimate since, as originally conceived, it attempted to get behind the creeds to " facts " which everyone, believer and unbeliever alike, would be compelled to
accept. It wrongly tried to substitute for faith the *bruta
facta* of Jesus' ministry. Robinson's quest is also new in
trying to go beyond not only this original quest but also
beyond Bultmann himself. The new quest wishes to establish a more vigorous connection between the preaching of
Jesus and the preaching of the early church than Bultmann
had been willing to admit.

According to Robinson, the new quest is possible because
of the new understanding of both history and the self to
which modern historiography has led. This view reads history not in terms of objective, external events but according to the intention of those who participate in it. If intention can be deduced from action, we can describe the
subject's understanding of himself, his relation to himself,
to other men, to God, and to the world, and this is all the
" history " that we really need. At the same time it is just
such data that the kerygmatic presentation of the Gospels
has preserved for us in the case of Jesus. By using such data
in the fashion modern historiography directs, we are given
a second avenue of approach to Jesus not available since
the time of his original disciples. In addition to our encounter with him in the preaching of the church, which
has been possible all along, we can now expose ourselves to
his own understanding of existence as gleaned from the
Synoptic tradition. We can thus assure ourselves of the
concreteness of Jesus as a historical person in a legitimate
way. Such a boon should be eagerly grasped, all the more
since the initial proclamation about Jesus — the *kerygma*
itself — depends for its grounding upon the historicity of
Jesus, upon Jesus as known " in the flesh." This new quest
is thus not only possible and legitimate but imperative.

It is also quite fruitful. By pursuing the new quest as

Robinson recommends we may now see that the continuity between Jesus and the *kerygma*, between proclaimer and proclaimed, is validated. Such validation occurs, not at the developmental level of external event or personality or formal teaching, but at the deeper level of existential selfhood. Since we find the same understanding of existence in Jesus as in the *kerygma*, a decision with regard to it is also a decision with regard to him. This same understanding of existence may even be used to test the authenticity of the *kerygma* itself, in whatever form it may speak about Jesus or report his sayings as risen Lord.

Robinson's work in carrying through this task is of particular interest to us since it involves a judgment concerning the Beatitudes contrary to the one we have expressed. The full impact of this judgment is spelled out both in the book we have been discussing and the article entitled " The Formal Structure of Jesus' Message." By analyzing those traditions concerning Jesus that are now most widely accepted as probably authentic, Robinson discovers in Jesus' sayings a certain " structuring tendency." [1] When any one saying is examined it reveals this tendency in the form of a certain " eschatological polarity " [2] between the present and the future. This is only what one would expect from the thrust of Jesus' whole message which reflects " an overlapping of present and future due to the inbreaking of God's reign into the present." [3] This overlapping Robinson accepts as an established consensus of modern New Testament research on which it is therefore safe to build. Along with this temporal polarity, however, Robinson also detects a certain " material antithesis " that is not temporal.[4] This nontemporal contrast simply describes in a variety of ways what life is like before and after God's coming.

The crux of Robinson's contention is the way in which he deals with these two contrasts, the temporal and the nontemporal. He will not let them stand side by side, but claims that the temporal distinction loses its importance in favor of the nontemporal distinction. The material antithesis overcomes the eschatological polarity. What emerges is a certain dialectical tension, " which is itself a first attempt to give expression to the understanding of existence implicit at the center of Jesus' message." [5] What Jesus really wishes to say is just this: existence in the present is eschatologically conditioned. To exist in the present is to be sustained by God's coming in the present.

It was such an understanding of existence that Jesus offered to men. It was such an understanding that made his eschatology relevant. It was such an understanding of existence by which Jesus himself lived, i.e., by which his own selfhood was actualized and his person constituted. He believed that the action of God, though hidden in this aeon, is man's only guarantee of freedom. It was in this faith that Jesus went to the cross (Mark 8:35). It was in vindication of this faith that his disciples were able to proclaim his resurrection and install him as ruler of the universe. To accept this faith is to experience mystical union with Jesus to this very day.

In support of such a far-reaching analysis, the Beatitudes and Woes of Luke 6:20-21, 24-25, play a major part since their contrast between now and then is overshadowed by their repeated contrasts between hunger and fullness, weeping and laughter. These latter contrasts are what Robinson means by a nontemporal " material antithesis." Here, if ever, according to his reading of the data, it is this emphasis that triumphs. According to Robinson, the Beatitudes do not then tell us about Jesus' sharp awareness of God's inbreaking rule to be completed only on the Last Day by a thorough reversal of existing conditions. Instead their dialectical tension simply reveals that real existence in the present depends on God's constant, direct support of the lowly. This is really the secret of Jesus' whole ministry. " God forgives the tax collectors and prostitutes; he breaks the security of the wealthy. . . . Within poverty is God's reign, within hunger fullness, among tears joy, whereas the full starve, and laughter becomes weeping and wailing. The self-saving life loses itself, while he who opens himself without reserve even to the extent of death lives all the while from God. Those who puff themselves up are brought down hard, but the lowly are borne by God. . . . In this eschatological occurrence, taking place in Jesus' present, his existence is constituted. This existence finds expression in various ways, but within the variety of expression there is a consistent interpretation of existence." [6]

Although a much fuller discussion of Robinson's interpretation would be in order, we must content ourselves with the posing of two questions. First, by what canon is it possible simply to erase the temporal thrust of Jesus' teaching? That both temporal and nontemporal stand side by side might indicate that each has its own contribution to make, each supporting and giving relevance to the other. Was Jesus' perception of reality actually as one-sided as Robinson pretends? It would seem particularly hazardous to eliminate the temporal aspect of Jesus' blessing. If Isa. 61:1-2 lies behind his blessing of the poor, the implication would seem to be that this blessing was a new act of God, inaugurating a new age not seen before (Luke 4:18; 6:20; 7:22-23). It is in keeping with this perspective that Jesus may be linked with the Baptist (Matt. 11:11-15) and contrasted with the prophets of old (Luke 10:23-24). It is in this light that one must see the newness of Jesus' triumph over Satan with all its attendant blessing (Mark 3:27; Matt. 12:28; Luke 10:17-20). When we consult such contemporary eschatology as we find at Qumran rather than the philosophical distinctions proper to existentialist analysis, the Synoptic tradition so interpreted in its first century setting gives us no reason to believe that Jesus repudiated a chronological tension between present and future. His correction of Qumran hardly implies a repudiation of its historical orientation.

Robinson's willingness to eliminate the temporal aspect of Jesus' teaching is even more perplexing since he himself recognizes that Jesus saw in the Baptist a historical turning point in God's coming to Israel, so that his situation, like that of the later church, was also temporally conditioned.[7] In an earlier article on the eschatological parables he also finds some such reference to a historical *terminus a quo,* apparently in Jesus' own ministry. " The parables look not only forward, but also backward. The hearer finds himself placed between the already-historical and the not-yet-historical, and is called upon to see, in the former, confirmation of the latter." [8] Although such a " prophetic concept of history " does not eliminate " history as resultant upon human decision," it gives to one's decision for God a historical rootage and focus.[9] Apparently in this instance Robinson is content to let the temporal and the nontemporal lie down in peace, the one supporting and complementing the other. So he comments about the parable of the marriage feast, " the feast is there, and someone must eat it. The preparation of the meal brings things to a head, introducing a situation of crisis and setting off the action of the narrative." [10] Likewise the parables of growth challenge Jesus' hearers to decision by putting them in " mid-season " [11] between a seed already sown and a harvest not yet reaped. Under these circumstances " the call for decision is a call for faith in the promise of history. Since the situation does not consist simply in anticipating a not-yet-historical event dominantly unambiguous in nature, but rather is based upon antecedent historical event, it should be, normally, conceived of as chronologically defined — not merely based upon but also subsequent to the *terminus a quo* — and chronological order becomes a theological problem (cf. Rom. 3:25 f.) ." [12]

To all of this one is prompted to respond with a hearty

amen! But why not then interpret the Beatitudes in a similar fashion as representing a tension between the historical
call of Jesus in the present of God's new age and the not
yet historical denouement toward which it points? How
else may we do justice to the sharp temporal contrast of
Luke's Beatitudes, which, far from being eliminated, is
rather repeated in his Woes?

A second question concerning Robinson's position is
more basic. If the Beatitudes are interpreted *only* in nontemporal terms as a clue to Jesus' understanding of existence, do we not thereby shift our focus from him to his
teaching? If what the Beatitudes tell us is that Jesus taught
and experienced a new understanding of existence that we
also ought to experience, then their importance lies in the
way of life they describe and not in the fact that Jesus at
a particular moment in history expressed through them a
new impetus toward the unfolding of God's purpose for
mankind. If the Beatitudes simply introduce us to a way
of lowliness dependent upon God's constant and direct
support, they cannot bear the weight put upon them by existentialist interpretation. Have we not found a similar
stance, a similar reading of God, man, and the world, in
both the canonical and the Qumran Psalters? Does not an
understanding of existence similar in kind meet us, for example, in the prophet Jeremiah (Jer. 15:15-21)? If Paul
had been an existentialist philosopher, would he not have
found in Abraham much the same kind of existential selfhood as Robinson finds in Jesus (Rom. 4:18-21)? If Jesus
expresses, albeit in a unique way, what we must identify
in all honesty as a traditional Jewish apprehension of God
and if this is the sum of his contribution to us, we may be
thankful indeed but we do not thereby have reason to exalt
him as the *kerygma* does. Then he becomes simply a striking illustration of a commendable way of life but only one
among many such illustrations which we may take or leave
as inclination dictates. Only when Jesus' blessing points be-

yond him to God's once-for-all activity through him may
we comprehend the importance of the blessing itself. It is
precisely the temporal thrust of the Beatitudes that accomplishes just this result. By setting men between God's new
age now present in Jesus and its unambiguous outcome in
the future, this reference to time actually illuminates
God's purpose for the whole world and gives Jesus his
rightful place as the once-for-all mediator of that purpose.

Apparently we must take more seriously than existentialist interpretation is willing to do the interest of both Jesus
and his followers in the activity of God, whether this be
fully understood or not (as at Pentecost, for example, Acts
2:22-36). Jesus affirmed God's fresh action in his own ministry. On the basis of his resurrection the church affirmed
God's action in their history. The line of continuity between proclaimer and proclaimed would seem to lie where
the whole New Testament puts it, in the activity of God.
Such continuity surely does not lie in man's ability to understand or communicate what God has done. Such understanding, according to the witness of the New Testament, usually lags far behind the encounter it attempts to
explain, and this too is in God's hands (cf. John, chs. 13 to
16, in particular, chs. 13:12; 16:12-15; cf. also I Cor., chs.
1 and 2, in particular, chs. 1:13, 30; 2:12-13). Thus is it not
Jesus' understanding of his death nor the church's understanding of it that lifts it from natural fact to eschatological reality. This is accomplished only by God's use of Jesus'
death to effect his plan of salvation for the whole world
(Rom. 3:21-26; Heb. 10:1-18). If existentialism directs attention to other more peripheral matters, however proper
in their own place, this would simply mean that its net is
too loosely woven to seize firmly the primary concerns of
Christian faith. Its method would not be an adequate tool
to bring resolution to the task assigned it.

The historical continuity that gives meaning to Christian faith is better described by Jeremias in his important

essay entitled *The Problem of the Historical Jesus.* According to Jeremias, we have in Jesus the unrepeatable, absolutely indispensable call of God, whereas in the witness of the early church we have what follows but is not equal in importance to this call, namely, their response. Call and response are related in the purpose of God, but to the call only may we assign priority.[13]

THE NEW HERMENEUTIC

As most readers will have guessed, Bultmann's interpretation of eschatology and Robinson's enthusiasm for the " new quest " rest ultimately on the so-called " new hermeneutic," a new formulation of the task of interpreting the New Testament. This, too, Bultmann and his students have been influential in developing.

Most interpreters of the New Testament would agree that four steps must be taken to ensure the completion of their task: (1) literary analysis, (2) historical investigation, (3) an exercise of personal sympathy toward the material to be interpreted, (4) a willingness to correct one's own questions and intentions by the questions and intentions of the text. Although he affirms the first two steps, Bultmann has given special attention to the last two. He enunciates four axioms: (*a*) Every interpreter comes to the text with some sort of prior understanding. (*b*) This he must subject to confrontation with the text. (*c*) Such confrontation can only take place at the level of existential analysis since the basic question posed by the New Testament is that of existence itself. (*d*) The relevant understanding of existence needed by the interpreter in this instance can only be had by putting himself into the hands of some such professional philosopher as Martin Heidegger. Since none of us can understand human existence, man as he really is in his being, without recourse to some sort of philosophical categories, it is imperative to make clear what these are. Heidegger offers expert guidance.

It is impossible here even to indicate the massive challenge such a proposal has laid down or the depth and extent of the discussion it has aroused. Once again it is to be hoped that the attentive reader will make some beginnings here for himself by a vigorous use of the bibliography. Suffice it to say that the debate occasioned by Bultmann's initial proposal raised questions no interpreter can avoid, especially as they are stated and restated with increasing clarity by students of Bultmann such as Ernst Fuchs and Gerhard Ebeling. As such men approach their task we find them pressing such queries as these: Does the New Testament text speak about objective external events or is the whole of its speech directed to arousing the response of its readers? Does it say, for example, that with Jesus the Messianic time has been brought by God or that the " time of self-understanding " has come? How do the New Testament authors understand themselves in relation to God and history; in what " world " do they actually move, and what challenge does this present to the self-understanding of the interpreter? Can the interpreter ever stand outside his text? Must he not always recognize that he too is a subject addressed in his own weakness by the text? Must he not only put questions to the text but answer the questions it puts to him, since the text is itself a " language event," an event by which God opens to man the possibility of authentic existence?

Let it be confessed here that such concerns are insistent. The interpreter has indeed a moral obligation to give them a hearing. Although we feel that the methods and scope of existential analysis are too narrow to do justice to the message presented by the New Testament, we must deal with the problems that it demands we confront. By way of illustrating this we allude for a moment now to the interpretation given to the Beatitudes by Luther and Wesley. The very contrast between them, not to mention the contrast between them and us, should give us a fitting sense of perspective when it comes to weighing our own presuppositions and opening these to confrontation with our text. If we find Luther and Wesley caught in the trap of their own world view, motivated by a desire to have their questions answered first, perhaps it may help us to formulate the proper questions for our study of this same text.

In short, there is a so-called " hermeneutic circle " that no interpreter, existentialist or otherwise, can possibly escape. Whether we like it or not, we cannot remove ourselves from the particular place given us on this earth. The best we can do is to recognize what our total situation really is and to ask what changes in it the text would suggest. If we are willing to listen and obey, we may then return to the text for further wisdom, thus renewing our quest and ourselves at the same time in a never ending cycle. The Christian interpreter, of course, will come to his task both to test and increase his faith. Such coming will always involve fresh receptivity to the Spirit, fresh appropriation of the risen Christ, and a more vigorous attempt to serve God in love. Seeing now " in a mirror dimly " we look forward to a " face to face " encounter. Knowing now " in part," we look forward to full understanding, in the faith that God understands us better than we shall ever understand either him or ourselves (I Cor. 13:12) .

LUTHER AND WESLEY

Luther's sermons on the Sermon were preached between 1530 and 1532 at Wittenberg. No one can read far in them without noticing his bitter polemic against both the Catholic church and the Anabaptists. Both this polemic and the resulting interpretation Luther gives to Matthew's Sermon are based on three fundamental axioms: (*a*) God has created certain stations for the common life of all men, Christian and pagan alike. (*b*) Faith in Christ is the indispensable source of all good works. (*c*) Every such axiom can be deduced only from the Word of God. By this latter Luther meant not simply the Old and the New Testaments but the constant activity of the God whom they reveal. When we take up Luther's exposition of the Beatitudes we recognize at once how pervasive is the influence of these special presuppositions.

The poor are blessed not because they are physically poor. " No one is blessed, therefore, because he is a beggar and owns nothing of his own. The command is to be ' spiritually poor.' I said at the very beginning that Christ is not dealing here at all with the secular realm and order, but that He wants to discuss only the spiritual — how to live before God above and beyond the external. Having money, property, honor, power, land, and servants belongs to the secular realm; without these it could not endure. Therefore a lord or prince should not and cannot be poor, because for his office and station he must have all sorts of goods like these." [14]

What it means to mourn is simply to accept the hardship that attends anyone who tries to do his Christian duty in his particular station in full dependence on God. " Therefore simply begin to be a Christian, and you will soon find out what it means to mourn and be sorrowful. If you can do nothing else, then get married, settle down, and make a living in faith. Love the Word of God and do what is required of you in your station. Then you will experience, both from your neighbors and in your own household, that things will not go as you might wish. You will be hindered and hemmed in on every side, so that you will suffer enough and see enough to make your heart sad." [15]

As we should expect, " righteousness " is defined by Luther in quite specific terms. It is not " that principal Christian righteousness by which a person becomes pious and acceptable to God." [16] That is, it is not the righteousness that comes by faith as a gift, on the basis of which one is

constituted a Christian. Rather, like all the other virtues
of the eight Beatitudes, it is simply a good work the like of
which only a Christian justified by faith can perform. Having applied this axiom Luther now proceeds to apply another by narrowing the scope of this particular righteousness to fit the special needs of his hearers. " Therefore," he
says, " take this in the sense of the outward righteousness
before the world, which we maintain in our relations with
each other. What is the righteousness of the world except
that in his station everyone should do his duty? That means
that the rights of every station should be respected — those
of the man, the woman, the child, the manservant, and the
maid in the household, the citizen of the city in the land." [17]
Of particular importance to Luther was the way in which a
Christian preacher should hunger and thirst after righteousness by performing his office with zeal. " The command to you is not to crawl into a corner or into the des-
ert, but to run out, if that is where you have been, and to
offer your hands and your feet and your whole body, and
to wager everything you have and can do. . . . If you cannot make the world completely pious, then do what you
can." [18] By way of contrast with this zeal of the Reformers,
Luther blasts away at Catholic monkery for its practice of
withdrawal from the world. His polemic is pointed. " The
counterfeit saints are exactly the opposite. Because of their
great sanctity they forsake the world and run into the des-
ert, or they sneak away into a corner somewhere, to escape
the trouble and worry that they would otherwise have to
bear. They do not want to pay attention to what is going
on in the world." [19]

When John Wesley set out to guide the people who had
responded to his preaching he relied not only on certain
Articles of Religion but also on his sermons and certain
notations on the New Testament that he had prepared
himself. He wanted to be both practical and Scriptural.
The sermons were intended to illustrate the spirit in which

the creed was to be understood, and the notes were intended to lay the groundwork for the sermons. Among the standard sermons thus recommended by Wesley were thirteen dealing with the entire Sermon on the Mount, the first three, expounding the Beatitudes, having been first preached around 1739. Wesley offered all thirteen sermons to his people as the basic norm for Christian ethics but so interpreted the Beatitudes as to make them the touchstone by which this norm should be controlled.

To state it briefly, the Beatitudes serve two purposes. They set forth those qualities of spirit which will characterize every true Christian. They also are arranged in climactic order to indicate the steps by which a Christian becomes what he ought to be. They are a kind of ladder by the climbing of which a Christian finally arrives at what Wesley called Christian perfection. Wesley thought of them as given directly by Jesus in just their present order to serve just this purpose. As he finishes his exposition of the Beatitudes, Wesley cries out, " Behold Christianity in its native form, as delivered by its great Author! This is the genuine religion of Jesus Christ! " [20]

To be poor in spirit means not to endure poverty but to repent. " Poverty of spirit then, as it implies the first step we take in running the race which is set before us, is a just sense of our inward and outward sins, and of our guilt and helplessness. This some have monstrously styled ' the virtue of humility'; thus teaching us to be proud of knowing we deserve damnation! But our Lord's expression is quite of another kind; conveying no idea to the hearer, but that of mere want, of naked sin, of helpless guilt and misery." [21] This is Wesley's approach to justification by faith. " One cannot but observe here, that Christianity begins just where heathen morality ends; poverty of spirit, conviction of sin, the renouncing ourselves, the not having our own righteousness (the very first point in the religion of Jesus Christ), leaving all pagan religion behind." [22]

Whereas Luther somewhat separates justifying faith from the Sermon as its already assumed foundation, Wesley finds justifying faith itself in this first Beatitude.

If Wesley differs from Luther on this score, he also puts the " righteousness " of the text in a different setting. Luther views each Beatitude as something of a test, i.e., he lets each Beatitude test the form that outward righteousness should take in the various stations of life. Wesley by contrast makes of righteousness a major rung in the ladder of Christian growth. It must be preceded by other virtues and itself is necessary to the attainment of further and full perfection.

The way in which Wesley describes this growth as the spiritual autobiography of every Christian is fascinating indeed. After the joy of initial repentance comes the sorrow induced by unexpected temptations. Then a true Christian will mourn both for his own sins and those of others. Such mourning brings comfort, and those who are so comforted soon discover in themselves a new meekness of spirit. This meekness expresses itself as " resignation " toward God, " patience " under trial and " gentleness " toward evil.[23] Such meek folk inherit the earth by being satisfied with everything they have. But when they arrive at this stage they are prepared for another. What is at stake here we must let Wesley describe directly. " Our Lord has hitherto been more immediately employed in removing the hindrances of true religion: such is pride, the first grand hindrance of all religion, which is taken away by poverty of spirit; levity and thoughtlessness, which prevent any religion from taking root in the soul, till they are removed by holy mourning: such are anger, impatience, discontent, which are all healed by Christian meekness. And when once these hindrances are removed, these evil diseases of the soul, which were continually raising false cravings therein, and filling it with sickly appetites, the native appetite of a heaven-born spirit returns; it hungers and thirsts after righteousness: and ' blessed are they which do hunger and thirst after righteousness: for they shall be filled.' " [24] Such righteousness begets both mercy and purity of heart which are the essence of Christian love. Fortified within by this love a true Christian will become a tireless peacemaker among all sorts and conditions of men in the world and be ready to endure the inevitable barbs of persecution that the world has reserved for him.

THREE UNANSWERED QUESTIONS ONCE AGAIN

As will be obvious by this time, we do feel that it is possible to get back to the historical Jesus, though not in the way envisaged by the " old quest." It should also be obvious that for us the methods of the " new quest " are too narrowly conceived. Perhaps some such pathway between the two as has been sketched in a recent essay by Heinrich Ott would represent the only course open for the moment.[25] But how has this appeared to us in nontechnical terms as we have pursued our studies? We may sum up as follows:

1. None of us can escape the relativities of historical existence. No reading of the past can establish uninterpreted facts nor proceed without choosing somewhere at some time some standpoint whose " guarantee " is the ultimate faith of the interpreter himself. The quest of the historical Jesus, both old and new, should have taught us this!

2. We need not despair at the limitations imposed upon us by such relativities and ambiguities.

a. We are given our place as interpreters within a historical continuum in this twentieth century where it is possible to test more widely now than ever before the various angles of vision by which Jesus has been viewed. Both the old quest and the new are in this sense a great boon, not a waste of effort but an invitation to further study.

b. The experience of the primitive church should also

encourage rather than discourage us. If our study of Matthew and Luke has been at all justified in its conclusions, not even those who stood closest to the primary event either could escape or desired to escape from the burden of interpretation. In continuing to interpret the interpreters we are simply following the path that has been marked out by them.

c. As Christians we may carry with us the faith of the first interpreters that the purpose of our work is not to establish a final and absolute certainty that can stand above the ambiguities of history. Is it not their witness to us that such certainty belongs only to God himself? This, if anything, we may learn from the acknowledged fact that they never separate the " historical Jesus " from their proclamation of him as risen Lord. Even Bultmann recognizes that the *kerygma* proclaimed a historical person whose " that-ness " was essential to its validation. Does not this unashamed combination of " interpretation " and " fact " on the part of the primitive church express its faith that, after all, the meaning of Jesus lies only in the continuing activity of God? If we accept such a hermeneutical standpoint, we need not weep and lament if our results are more meager than we had hoped and our certainties less certain. If we accept such a standpoint we need not fix our decision between Jesus and the *kerygma* in so binding an " either-or " vise. We need not insist as the old questers do that salvation lies *only* with the " historical Jesus." Nor need we say with Bultmann that we can encounter Jesus *only* in the preaching of the primitive church or in our preaching. We make room for *both* Jesus *and* the *kerygma,* both the Proclaimer and the Proclaimed, realizing that each in his own way has his contribution to make to the ultimate purpose of God. Relying on the riches given us by both quests, grounding our efforts in the interpretive activity of the first generation of Christians, we commit our results with all their ambiguities into the hands of God, knowing that he will use them as he sees fit, just as he has in every generation preceding.

3. If our position as interpreters is God's gift to us in Christ, we must then be prepared to exercise the freedom with which he has set us free. Since this freedom is real our interpretation must not consist simply in repeating what we have received. This wooden concept of the interpretive role ignores the particular responsibilities put upon us to speak God's word in our time and in our tongue to the needs of our own generation. We may learn here not only from Matthew and Luke but also from Luther and Wesley, not to mention our Lord himself. In this respect the Evangelists and the Reformers are his servants, exhibiting his gift of freedom to them.

We have already tried to exhibit such freedom ourselves in the answering of three unanswered questions. In our reading of Jesus' intent we used the contrary witness of Matthew and Luke to re-create such an image of him as seemed right from our own standpoint. We did not insist on the words of either Evangelist as the exact words of Jesus. Acting in the power of this freedom we tried to let Luke speak for himself in his own right concerning proclamation, vindication, and sovereignty. Although not ignoring Matthew's emphasis on discipleship, we refused to make Luke conform to this pattern. We have not hesitated to break up the precise combinations of material found in each Gospel in order to shift its focus and revise its context, claiming that Jesus gave his blessing to differing groups on differing occasions and with differing intent. In the light of the Sitz-im-Leben revealed by both source criticism and form criticism, as well as by our historically grounded word studies, this is what we had to do. In the next chapter we shall carry this freedom further by suggesting certain axioms for modern preaching based upon the insights thus gained.

Meanwhile we must keep in mind one further aspect of

our situation. Since our freedom to interpret is not our own creation, it is limited. It is a gift given to us as Christians within a context created by Jesus' life, death, resurrection, and continuing presence. If we therefore acknowledge his Lordship by faith, we must confess that our interest in this quest is one dictated by faith itself. We must know as much of his historical image as possible since our whole existence as human beings depends so completely on what he has done for us. Beyond these limits we cannot go. What we present to those who may disagree with us must be presented as from faith to faith. We must speak not as though delivering a final and absolute word gained solely by reason of specialized study but simply as humble servants bearing such witness as God in Christ has commanded us to bear.

NOTES *

1. James M. Robinson, "The Formal Structure of Jesus' Message," *Current Issues in New Testament Interpretation,* ed. by William Klassen and Graydon F. Snyder (Harper & Row, Publishers, Inc., 1962), p. 97.

2. *Ibid.,* p. 98.

3. *Ibid.,* pp. 98–99.

4. *Ibid.,* p. 98.

5. *Ibid.,* p. 99.

6. *Ibid.,* p. 104.

7. James M. Robinson, *A New Quest of the Historical Jesus* (Studies in Biblical Theology, No. 25; Alec R. Allenson, Inc., 1959), p. 119.

8. James M. Robinson, "Jesus' Understanding of History," *The Journal of Bible and Religion,* XXIII (January, 1955), p. 19.

9. *Ibid.*

10. *Ibid.,* p. 22.

11. *Ibid.,* p. 23.

*Books listed here are not duplicated in the bibliography.

12. *Ibid.*
13. Joachim Jeremias, *The Problem of the Historical Jesus* (Facet Books, Biblical Series, No. 13; Fortress Press, 1964), pp. 22–24.
14. Jaroslav Pelikan, ed., *Luther's Works,* Vol. 21: *The Sermon on the Mount and the Magnificat* (Concordia Publishing House, 1956), p. 12.
15. *Ibid.,* p. 20.
16. *Ibid.,* p. 26.
17. *Ibid.*
18. *Ibid.,* p. 27.
19. *Ibid.,* p. 28.
20. Edward H. Sugden, ed., *Wesley's Standard Sermons,* Vol. I (London: The Epworth Press, 1921), p. 377.
21. *Ibid.,* p. 325.
22. *Ibid.,* p. 326.
23. *Ibid.,* p. 337.
24. *Ibid.,* p. 342.
25. Heinrich Ott, "The Historical Jesus and the Ontology of History," *The Historical Jesus and the Kerygmatic Christ,* ed. and tr. by Carl E. Braaten and Roy A. Harrisville (Abingdon Press, 1964), pp. 142–171. See also Richard R. Niebuhr, *Resurrection and Historical Reason,* Ch. III, "The Possibility of an Historical Reason" (Charles Scribner's Sons, 1957).

BIBLIOGRAPHY

BULTMANN AND THE NEW QUEST

Anderson, Hugh, *Jesus and Christian Origins: A Commentary on Modern Viewpoints.* Oxford University Press, Inc., 1964.
Bornkamm, Günther, *Jesus of Nazareth,* tr. by Irene and Fraser McLusky with James M. Robinson. Harper & Brothers, 1961.
Bultmann, Rudolf, *Jesus and the Word,* tr. by Louise P. Smith and Erminie H. Lantero. Paperback. Charles Scribner's Sons, 1958.
—— *Theology of the New Testament,* Vol. I, tr. by Kendrick Grobel. Charles Scribner's Sons, 1954.
Fuchs, Ernst, *Studies of the Historical Jesus,* tr. by Andrew

Scobie (Studies in Biblical Theology, No. 42). Alec R. Allenson, Inc., 1964.

Käsemann, Ernst, *Essays on New Testament Themes* (Studies in Biblical Theology, No. 41). Alec R. Allenson, Inc., 1964.

Piper, Otto, "A Unitary God with Jesus as His First Theologian," *Interpretation*, XV (October, 1961), pp. 473–483. A review of *Jesus of Nazareth* by Günther Bornkamm.

Robinson, James M., "The Historical Jesus and the Church's Kerygma," *Religion in Life*, 26 (1956), pp. 40–49.

—— "The Recent Debate on the 'New Quest,'" *The Journal of Bible and Religion*, XXX (July, 1962), pp. 198–208.

The New Hermeneutic

Bartsch, Hans W. (ed.), *Kerygma and Myth: A Theological Debate,* tr. by R. H. Fuller. London: S. P. C. K.; Vol. I, 1957, Vol. II, 1962.

Braaten, Carl E., and Harrisville, Roy A. (eds. and trs.), *Kerygma and History: A Symposium on the Theology of Rudolf Bultmann.* Abingdon Press, 1962.

Bultmann, Rudolf, "Is Exegesis Without Presuppositions Possible?" *Existence and Faith,* tr. and intro. by Schubert Ogden. Living Age Book 29. Meridian Books, Inc., 1960.

—— *Jesus Christ and Mythology.* Charles Scribner's Sons, 1958.

Ebeling, Gerhard, *The Nature of Faith,* tr. by Ronald G. Smith. Muhlenberg Press, 1961.

—— *Word and Faith,* tr. by James W. Leitch. Fortress Press, 1963.

Funk, R. W., "Colloquium on Hermeneutics," *Theology Today,* XXI (October, 1964), pp. 287–306.

Henderson, Ian, *Myth in the New Testament* (Studies in Biblical Theology, No. 7), Alec R. Allenson, Inc., 1952.

Ogden, Schubert M., *Christ Without Myth.* Harper & Brothers, 1961.

Robinson, James M., and Cobb, John B. (eds.), *The New Hermeneutic.* Harper & Row, Publishers, Inc., 1964.

Throckmorton, Burton H., *The New Testament and Mythology.* The Westminster Press, 1959.

Weber, Joseph C., "Language-Event and Christian Faith," *Theology Today,* XXI (January, 1965), pp. 449–457.

THE OLD QUEST (RESUMED) *

Baird, J. Arthur, *The Justice of God in the Teaching of Jesus.* The Westminster Press, 1963.

Case, S. J., *Jesus, A New Biography.* The University of Chicago Press, 1927.

Goguel, Maurice, *The Life of Jesus,* tr. by Olive Wyon. The Macmillan Company, 1944. Now available in two volumes as a paperback. Harper Torchbooks TB 65 and TB 66.

Rowlingson, Donald, "The Focal Point of Faith: Jesus or Tradition?" *The Journal of Bible and Religion,* XXXI (January, 1963), pp. 17–22.

Stauffer, Ethelbert, *Jesus and His Story,* tr. by Richard and Clara Winston. Alfred A. Knopf, Inc., 1960.

THE HISTORY OF INTERPRETATION

Grant, Robert M., *A Short History of the Interpretation of the Bible,* rev. ed. Paperback 137. The Macmillan Company, 1963.

McArthur, Harvey K., *Understanding the Sermon on the Mount.* Harper & Brothers, 1960.

Neill, Stephen C., *The Interpretation of the New Testament 1861–1961.* London: Oxford University Press, 1964.

THE CONTINUING TASK OF INTERPRETATION

Barrett, C. K., *Biblical Problems and Biblical Preaching.* Facet Books, Biblical Series, No. 6. Fortress Press, 1964.

Barth, Markus, *Conversation with the Bible.* Holt, Rinehart and Winston, Inc., 1964.

Blackman, E. C., *Biblical Interpretation.* The Westminster Press, 1959.

Cadbury, Henry J., *The Peril of Modernizing Jesus.* The Macmillan Company, 1937.

Harrisville, Roy, *His Hidden Grace: The Origins, Task and Witness of Biblical Criticism.* Abingdon Press, 1965.

*See further examples in Jeremias, *The Problem of the Historical Jesus.*

Herbert, Arthur G., *The Christ of Faith and the Jesus of History*. Alec R. Allenson, Inc., 1962.

Knox, John, *Criticism and Faith*. Abingdon-Cokesbury Press, 1952.

—— *Jesus: Lord and Christ*. Harper & Brothers, 1958.

Lindars, Barnabas, *New Testament Apologetic*. The Westminster Press, 1961.

Piper, Otto, *God in History*. The Macmillan Company, 1939.

—— "Principles of New Testament Interpretation," *Theology Today*, III (1946), pp. 192–204.

Reicke, Bo, "Incarnation and Exaltation: The Historic Jesus and the Kerygmatic Christ," *Interpretation*, XVI (1962), pp. 156–168.

Wilder, Amos N., *The Language of the Gospel: Early Christian Rhetoric*. Harper & Row, Publishers, Inc., 1964.

—— *Otherworldliness and the New Testament*. Harper & Brothers, 1954.

VIII · Some Axioms for Modern Preaching

NOW THAT WE HAVE COME SO FAR FROM THE FIRST QUESTIONS we put to our text we must not forget what we have learned in the process of seeking an answer. Although we must now exercise freedom in speaking as directly as we can to the particular needs of our own time, it is part of the limitation put upon our freedom that we must not forget what we have learned. We have no right whatsoever to speak as Christian interpreters apart from such a struggle as we have just experienced. Only by standing as fully as we have tried to stand within the continuum of Christian history have we any right to proclaim its glad mystery. We have listened to Matthew and Luke and to their nameless forebears in the formation of the tradition both Jewish and Christian. We have listened to Luther and Wesley and to a whole host of contemporary interpreters. Above all, by interpreting these interpreters, we have sought to hear the voice of Jesus. We are now free to move out on our own but our freedom has been hard won and its fruits must not be neglected or surrendered.

What have we learned from the Beatitudes of Jesus? Chiefly this, that God's blessing is his to give in his own time and his own way to whomsoever he wills. This is to say that his blessing always comes in an eschatological setting. It has no meaning apart from what he is doing in the world to bring his sovereign purpose to its intended fruition. From his own he invites personal obedience and to them he promises vindication both here and hereafter. Beyond his own, in the broad reaches of creation that also belong to him as the Lord God Almighty, he vindicates whom he will as his mercy and justice demand. No man can stay his hand. This we know because once in history he spoke and acted once for all in his Son. We listen to him and we ask all men so to listen since God's blessing is Christ's alone to give. However differently they develop its meaning, both Evangelists are unmistakably moved by this burning certainty.

Facing the demands he puts upon us now and the needs by which he beckons us to serve our fellowmen, we find in the blessing of God's Son three urgent words. For the old decaying aeon in whose midst we live there is a word of warning. For those who stand in the acknowledged company of God's Son, in lowliness awaiting his return, there is a word of invitation and promise. For those whose gift it is to interpret the mystery of God's will there is a word of caution lest in speaking of God's blessing carelessly we encourage our brethren to believe that they can earn it on their own, apart from God's Son.

FOR THE SOCIAL ORDER: A WORD OF JUDGMENT

Here we draw quite obviously on the Lucan version of the Beatitudes according to which Jesus proclaims to his generation, out of his intimate communion with God and his keen knowledge of his own times, that something is amiss which only God himself can put right. The result will be a complete reversal of the present world order. Taught here by the Old Testament, by Luke, and even to some degree by our comparisons with Qumran we do not stop to debate whether Jesus spoke to the poor or to the poor in spirit. We move through these distinctions to the eschatological context in which they are lodged in order to see what Jesus wants us to see — God the Creator at work in the midst of his creation.

In speaking thus with corporate and cosmic reference, Jesus reveals how profoundly he thinks and lives as a child of the Old Testament. It is in the Old Testament that we find the God to whom Jesus appeals. He is the creator of all things, in heaven, on earth, and under the earth. He calls men and nations into being and when they rebel against his will he puts his fish hook into their mouth and leads them about like great dragons, trembling and obedient before their maker. So he did to Egypt, beginning with Pharoah (Isa., ch. 18). So he did to Sennacherib, King of Assyria (ch. 37). So he called Cyrus of Persia and humbled Nebuchadnezzar of Babylon (chs. 45:1 to 47:15). So he speaks through Amos to Damascus, " For three transgressions of Damascus, and for four, I will not revoke the punishment; because they have threshed Gilead with threshing sledges of iron. So I will send a fire upon the house of Hazael, and it shall devour the strongholds of Ben-hadad " (Amos 1:3-4). If God had used the nations round about Israel to chastise her for her sins and if they had in turn fallen victim to his wrath, why should not the same drama play itself out once again in the case of Rome? The thought at least was native to the air Jesus breathed as a child of the Old Testament.

Beyond this we remember that Jesus had identified himself with John the Baptist, and that John was a national figure in his own right. When he accused Herod openly because of his liaison with Herodias, he was exercising an ancient prophetic function: to remind the kings of Israel that they were responsible to God. The anger of Herod was so intense because he knew full well that John's word had aroused the people against him. In Herod's eyes John was a potential rebel against the established order. The sequence of events as reported by Josephus brings this out quite clearly. After John was beheaded and Herod took

Herodias in place of his former wife he got himself into
even deeper troubles. Aretas, the father of his jilted wife,
whose kingdom bordered his own, set out to drive Herod
from his throne in revenge and was only stopped by Roman intervention. The fact that Aretas so nearly succeeded
in toppling Herod was not lost on the common people. According to Josephus, they interpreted Herod's near defeat
as God's judgment on him for his having beheaded the
Baptist.

Now it was in such a heated state of affairs that Jesus
openly sided with John and relied for his own defense
upon John's popularity with the people (Mark 11:27-33).
It is against such a background that Herod looks upon Jesus as John raised from the dead (ch. 6:16) and that Jesus
transfixes Herod forever with a memorable word of rebuke
(Luke 13:31-33). " At that very hour some Pharisees came
and said to him, ' Get away from here, for Herod wants to
kill you.' And he said to them, ' Go and tell that fox, " Behold, I cast out demons and perform cures today and tomorrow, and the third day I finish my course." ' " Here Jesus himself appears like John in the tradition of the Old
Testament prophets whose function made them responsible for national destiny. His stinging rebuke reflects the
traditional hostility between the prophet and the wicked
ruler and reveals in a momentary flash Jesus' deep insight
into both Herod's character and the insecurity of his political position. Indeed, as the object of Herod's ire, Jesus
becomes, like John before him, a marked man.

When we turn to consider Jesus' attitude toward Rome
we receive a similar impression of Jesus' sensitivity to the
cultural climate of Palestine. To be sure he was not what
we would call a political strategist with an interest in social
or economic reform, but he did phrase his message about
God so that people whose lives were ridden by these bur-
dens would know what he meant. Although we cannot
press his famous word about tribute to Caesar (Mark

12:13-17), at least it is clear that Jesus does not speak here like a Zealot intent on armed rebellion. Quite to the contrary he counsels compliance with Rome. Whoever is asked to carry a Roman pack one mile should carry it two (Matt. 5:41). More recently some scholars have suggested that v. 43 points in the same direction. Nowhere in our canonical Old Testament can a text be found that explicitly commands Jews to hate their enemies. Is it possible that Jesus is dealing here with a well-known militant interpretation of the Old Testament put forward by the Essenes and that he does so explicitly in order to draw its sting? We know that the Essenes at Qumran in this period had been influenced by the Zealots in their desire for open revolt against Rome. We also know that Jesus chose as two of his most intimate disciples, Levi the publican, a servant of Rome, and Simon the Zealot, a sworn enemy of Rome. Why should he have done this if not as a leader in Israel to dramatize his utter repudiation of the Zealot position?

But the climax of Jesus' career as a national figure comes in the manner of his death. In spite of his refusal to approve Zealot rebellion against Rome, in spite of his advice to turn the other cheek and go the second mile, he was put to death at the last on political charges at the hands of the Roman governor. Whatever Jesus' intentions, whether we label them political or religious in our sense of these words, he had in fact become a disturber of the peace. Whether by his criticism of the Pharisees, by his cleansing of the Temple, or by his preaching of judgment upon the city of Jerusalem, he challenged the status quo to its depths with such vigor that he had to be done away with. For whatever reason, the sober fact is that his enemies were able to set Jesus before Pilate as a Messianic pretender, as a fomenter of the armed rebellion he had all along discouraged. The details of his trial are no longer clear but its outcome is undisputed. That he should be executed as King of the Jews is testimony to the bruising impact that his ministry actually made on his nation's life.

When we draw together all these factors to which our study has pointed, the picture that emerges is striking indeed. Jesus appears as an Old Testament prophet who supports John's bold criticism of Herod and his dire prediction of judgment to come for the whole nation. He moves as did the prophets in the serene conviction that the God of Abraham, Isaac, and Jacob is able to root up and tear down the mightiest nations on earth. He himself draws the ire of Herod and sharply opposes armed rebellion against Rome both by word and by prophetic symbolism. He himself predicts the destruction of Jerusalem and announces the coming of God's rule in power. In the end he is crucified on political charges as a disturber of Rome's uneasy peace. What else can we say about him than that he threw down a decisive challenge to the whole of the social order in whose midst he walked? What more likely word could we have from his lips than " Blessed are you that weep now, for you shall laugh "?

The impact of this picture has been obscured in recent years by both the thorough-going eschatology of Schweitzer and the existentialism of Bultmann. If one follows these interpreters seriously, Jesus is either transported beyond history entirely or he is transformed into a Jewish saint whose only concern is with the individual in his moment of decision. By way of contrast the picture we have sketched follows, except for one major difference, the general orientation proposed by Amos Wilder. In his view the eschatological myth of Jesus speaks to men in the midst of their concrete social and political involvements. It does call for personal decision but it does so in the light of the new social order that God himself is bringing out of the ruins of the old. We are not as certain as Wilder that Jesus looked forward to a new social order on this earth. Jesus' imagery is not precise enough for this but suggests, rather, the coming of a whole new aeon whose nature transcends the conditions known to men on this planet.

On the other hand we are convinced that Jesus sent forth his blessing and woe to the men of his day in terms of the social, political, and economic tensions that they knew. Nothing bears witness to this with deeper eloquence than the way in which Jesus joins national doom to cosmic doom. In one of the oldest sources Jesus' word about the Son of Man is joined to his teaching about the fall of Jerusalem (Luke 17:22-31). In our view this would root Jesus' teaching about the final vindication of the suffering remnant where it belongs, in the history of Israel. It moves from the disintegration of Israel's life to the use God will make of it for the accomplishment of his eternal purpose. Apparently Jesus saw in the distressing events of his own time the prelude to the great renewal which he hoped that God would soon bring for his whole creation.

Can we hope for anything less in our time? Is it not God himself who is moving among us to destroy the patterns that our fathers knew? It cannot be happenstance that our way to the future is blocked by cold war, racial strife, and resurgent nationalism. As one pastor expressed it on his bulletin board in a time of great upheaval in his town, " The hunger for human rights is the gift of God." Just so, in the spirit of Jesus we may accept such unrest as a warning from God that we have not yet responded to him our Creator as we ought. With hope we may also believe, even beyond the horizons of Jesus, that God will vindicate his poor even on this earth.

FOR THE COMMITTED: AN INVITATION TO OBEY AND TO HOPE

We may well imagine Jesus saying to his most intimate followers what we find now in Matthew's interpretive redaction — " This is the way! Walk ye in it! " The Beatitudes would then be discipleship ethics, the ethics of obe-

dience. For those of us who know also the risen Lord their
impact would be doubled. For Christ has already experienced in the resurrection the vindication he promised so
that we may look forward with renewed hope to his com-
pleting what he has begun.

In making our response we need to remember that these
blessings are given to the whole people of God. We do not
stand alone. God himself in the call of his Son and the
sending of his Spirit has bound us together. This is the
way he meant it to be. The address of Jesus in Matthew's
version is to the group. They together are to be the successors to the prophets. So often we miss this note and by
isolating ourselves from each other make our obedience so
much the more difficult.

We must also be careful to put the demands of this ethic
in their proper light. So often we hear good people speak
of this ethic as impossible of achievement. Its purpose,
they say, is to humble us in the dust.[1] Of course this is
what does happen, but then this is exactly what we should
expect to happen! This is the word of the Messiah to his
people, and the Messiah in order to become such had to
die on the cross. We now live in a time when the Messiah
has yet to be recognized. He lives in his church and his
Word and his Sacraments incognito — not yet in glory but
in humiliation. Until that time of glory appears, why
should we wonder if it is his people's function to suffer
with him?

No one has put this better than Dietrich Bonhoeffer in
his book *The Cost of Discipleship.* " By ' mourning ' Jesus, of course, means doing without what the world calls
peace and prosperity: He means refusing to be in tune
with the world or to accommodate oneself to its standards.
Such men mourn for the world, for its guilt, its fate and its
fortune. While the world keeps holiday they stand aside,
and while the world sings ' Gather ye rose-buds while ye
may,' they mourn. They see that for all the jollity on

board, the ship is beginning to sink. The world dreams of progress, of power and of the future, but the disciples meditate on the end, the last judgment, and the coming of the kingdom. To such heights the world cannot rise. And so the disciples are strangers in the world, unwelcome guests and disturbers of the peace." [2]

For the Interpreter: A Word of Caution

We have maintained thus far that when the Beatitudes are addressed generally to the uncommitted, they should be formulated according to the Lucan pattern and that when they are addressed to disciples only, they should be rooted in the presuppositions of the framework given them by Matthew. It remains now to register a strong protest when these differing points of departure are ignored or confused or denied.

The point at issue is not theoretical but pastoral and practical. If we lay upon men the duty of fulfilling what the Beatitudes demand, we place upon them a burden they cannot bear. If we make such attainment a condition of enjoying God's presence, we exclude Christian and non-Christian alike from his Kingdom.

Hans Windisch felt this problem so acutely that he boldly refused to accept what he regarded as the pre-Christian legalism of the Sermon for himself, but insisted upon tempering it with postresurrection wisdom. Concerning the sixth Beatitude he writes: " Jesus restricts himself to the assurance that the pure in heart will see God in the new age, in God's Kingdom. But we know we cannot appear before God as we are, for our hearts are flecked with sin. We should perish — this is the judgment that hangs over us. So we expand the Beatitude: ' Blessed are those who have the Spirit of God, for they shall see God.' " [3] Martin Dibelius makes a similar protest in a different way. For him, the demands of the Sermon are so absolute that they cannot be applied directly to modern conditions of life. They are intended not to convert or condemn the world but to provide " an eschatological stimulus " that will alert men to " the pure will of God." [4] As such they are for Christians only and their purpose is to help such Christians to live in a more responsible way. By so living they will become what Jesus was, a " sign " of God's Kingdom. Although we have chosen with Bonhoeffer to solve our problem in a way that neither Dibelius nor Windisch have used, we have kept before us constantly this concern so prominent in the work of all three. We have analyzed Matthew's Sermon as presupposing the grace of God offered in Jesus and have seen the power to fulfill its demands as the gift of the risen Lord himself. In our reading, the implied demand of the Beatitudes becomes a test of our fellowship with God rather than a hurdle to be overcome in attaining that fellowship.

It is from this standpoint that we urge a word of caution upon those modern interpreters who, like Gerald Heard, openly address the Beatitudes to all men as a pathway toward self-salvation or who, like Ralph Sockman, fail to make clear whether the Beatitudes are basically a gift or a demand.

It is relatively easy to confront the forthright proposal of Heard with such an equally forthright position as that taken, for example, by John Wesley. Are the Beatitudes really a bridge of principle to be flung over the moat dividing believer from unbeliever? If they simply constitute a ladder of perfection to be ascended by any well-meaning man who will make the effort, we answer: " No! " If they lead to the acceptance of God's grace in Jesus before ever the first rung of the ladder is attempted, we answer: " Yes! " We say no to Gerald Heard and yes to John Wesley.

With *The Higher Happiness* of Dr. Sockman, the task of analysis is not so easy, since we cannot tell much of the time whether he wishes to follow Wesley or Heard! From one point of view his work deserves high praise. The Beatitudes are Jesus' word to his disciples only overheard by a reluctant and wistful world, but both presupposing the acceptance of God's sovereignty and demanding the experience of his grace.[5] Running side by side with this proposal is another line of argument no doubt intended to make clear how deeply the ethics of Jesus are written into the nature of human nature itself. According to this line of reasoning, the Beatitudes recommend those principles for living most highly prized by Jesus. Since God has so ordered the world that these principles can be realized and since they carry their own reward in this life, no sensible man will fail to strive to live by them. So we learn that to be meek is simply in the first instance to accept those restraints that everyone must endure just to survive. The meek are bound to triumph, since by practicing such restraint they get more out of themselves, out of others, and out of their environment.[6] Those who mourn so enter into the sufferings of others that they themselves do find comfort.[7] To recognize God in all things, one has only to concentrate on the good, the true, and the beautiful. It is in this sense that " the pure in heart," i.e., the single-minded, " see God." [8] Whatever Dr. Sockman intends, such divided counsel seems to put the initiative into our hands and sets us to wondering whether Christ's blessing is not just another pious name for our achievement.

Such counsel also fails to interpret Matthew. If we listen to Matthew, discipleship begins with Jesus and its rewards are his gift. Our effort does not deserve this reward, nor is the hope of receiving such reward ever made the incentive for our obedience. We obey because it is God's Son who has commanded us to do so. We are blessed, as were the original Twelve, because God sent his Son to save us in spite of our weakness and in the midst of continuing failure.

NOTES

1. Consult the treatment of John Knox, *The Ethic of Jesus in the Teaching of the Church.* Abingdon Press, 1961.

2. Dietrich Bonhoeffer, *The Cost of Discipleship,* p. 98.

3. H. Windisch, *The Meaning of the Sermon on the Mount,* p. 178.

4. M. Dibelius, *The Sermon on the Mount,* p. 135. For an illuminating review of this whole problem, the last two chapters of Dibelius should be compared with the last chapter of Windisch.

5. Ralph Sockman, *The Higher Happiness,* pp. 15–23, 47, 55–60, 111–116. Sockman agrees with Wesley that Matthew arranged his Beatitudes in climactic order! Cf. pp. 41, 77, 110–111, 155.

6. *Ibid.,* pp. 71–75.

7. *Ibid.,* pp. 49–55.

8. *Ibid.,* pp. 125–128.